"Daughter," He said to her,
"your faith has made you well.
Go in peace."

—

LUKE 8:48 HCSB

The quoted ideas expressed in this book (but not Scripture verses) are not, in all cases, exact quotations, as some have been edited for clarity and brevity. In all cases, the author has attempted to maintain the speaker's original intent. In some cases, quoted material for this book was obtained from secondary sources, primarily print media. While every effort was made to ensure the accuracy of these sources, the accuracy cannot be guaranteed. For additions, deletions, corrections, or clarifications in future editions of this text, please write Freeman-Smith.

The Holy Bible, King James Version

The Holy Bible, New King James Version (NKJV) Copyright © 1982 by Thomas Nelson, Inc. Used by permission.

New Century Version®. (NCV) Copyright © 1987, 1988, 1991 by Word Publishing, a division of Thomas Nelson, Inc. All rights reserved. Used by permission.

The Holman Christian Standard Bible™ (HCSB) Copyright © 1999, 2000, 2001 by Holman Bible Publishers. Used by permission.

The Holy Bible, New International Version®. (NIV) Copyright © 1973, 1978, 1984 International Bible Society. Used by permission of Zondervan. All rights reserved.

The Holy Bible. New Living Translation (NLT) copyright © 1996 Tyndale Charitable Trust. Used by permission of Tyndale House Publishers.

The New American Standard Bible®, (NASB) Copyright © 1960, 1962, 1963, 1968, 1971, 1972, 1973, 1975, 1977, 1995 by The Lockman Foundation. Used by permission.

Scripture taken from The Message. (MSG) Copyright © 1993, 1994, 1995, 1996, 2000, 2001, 2002. Used by permission of NavPress Publishing Group.

Cover Design by Kim Russell / Wahoo Designs
Page Layout by Bart Dawson

ISBN 978-1-60587-503-3

Printed in the United States of America

1 2 3 4 5—CHG—17 16 15 14 13

a
WOMAN'S
GARDEN
FAITH
of

TABLE OF CONTENTS

INTRODUCTION

The dictionary defines the word *garden* as "a plot of land used to grow flowers, fruits, or vegetables." This definition is correct, as far as it goes. But those of us who carefully cultivate our own little plots of God's good earth know that a garden is much more than a place for growing plants. It is also a place to renew our spirits as we commune with our Creator and marvel at the beauty of His creation.

Faith, like a garden, can be cultivated or neglected. When we nurture our faith through prayer, meditation, and worship, God enriches our lives and lifts our spirits. And, this book is intended to help. The ideas on these pages can help you cultivate your own "garden of faith." When you do, you will reap a rich harvest of spiritual blessings and a cornucopia of earthly rewards.

So, during the next thirty days, try this experiment: read one chapter a day and take the ideas in that chapter to heart. While you're at it, remember that your own faith in God, like a tender seedling, must be nurtured and protected. And, please remember that the most important seed you'll ever plant is the seed of Christ's love that you plant forever in your heart.

A WOMAN'S GARDEN OF FAITH

*For whatever is born of God overcomes the world.
And this is the victory that has
overcome the world—our faith.*

—

1 JOHN 5:4 NKJV

Welcome to the garden of faith, a place where you can plant the seed of hope in your heart and reap a bountiful harvest that is both timely and timeless.

A suffering woman sought healing in an unusual way: she simply touched the hem of Jesus' garment. When she did, Jesus turned and said, "Daughter, be of good comfort; thy faith hath made thee whole" (Matthew 9:22 KJV). We, too, can be made whole when we place our faith completely and unwaveringly in the person of Jesus Christ.

Concentration camp survivor Corrie ten Boom relied on faith during ten months of imprisonment and torture. Later, despite the fact that four of her family members had died in Nazi death camps, Corrie's faith was unshaken. She wrote, "There is no pit so deep that God's love is not deeper still." Christians take note: Genuine faith in God means faith in all circumstances, happy or sad, joyful or tragic.

When you place your faith, your trust, indeed your life in the hands of Christ Jesus, you'll be amazed at the marvelous things He can do with you and through you. So strengthen your faith through praise, through worship, through Bible study, and through prayer. Then, trust God's plans. He is standing at the door of your heart. If you reach out to Him in faith, He will give you peace and heal your broken spirit. Be content to touch even a fragment of the Master's garment, and He will make you whole.

PROMISES FROM GOD'S WORD

Now faith is the reality of what is hoped for, the proof of what is not seen.

HEBREWS 11:1 HCSB

Now without faith it is impossible to please God, for the one who draws near to Him must believe that He exists and rewards those who seek Him.

HEBREWS 11:6 HCSB

Indeed, God is my salvation. I will trust [Him] and not be afraid. Because Yah, the LORD, is my strength and my song, He has become my salvation.

ISAIAH 12:2 HCSB

A TIMELY TIP FROM THE GARDEN OF FAITH

Faith in God is contagious, and when it comes to your family's spiritual journey, no one's faith is more contagious than yours! Act, pray, praise, and trust God with the certain knowledge that every member of your family is watching . . . carefully!

MORE GREAT IDEAS

Just as our faith strengthens our prayer life, so do our prayers deepen our faith. Let us pray often, starting today, for a deeper, more powerful faith.

SHIRLEY DOBSON

There are a lot of things in life that are difficult to understand. Faith allows the soul to go beyond what the eyes can see.

JOHN MAXWELL

Grace calls you to get up, throw off your blanket of helplessness, and to move on through life in faith.

KAY ARTHUR

Faith is seeing light with the eyes of your heart, when the eyes of your body see only darkness.

BARBARA JOHNSON

Faith is trusting in advance what will only make sense in reverse.

PHILIP YANCEY

When you and I place our faith in Jesus Christ and invite Him to come live within us, the Holy Spirit comes upon us, and the power of God overshadows us, and the life of Jesus is born within us.

ANNE GRAHAM LOTZ

If God chooses to remain silent, faith is content.

RUTH BELL GRAHAM

Sometimes the very essence of faith is trusting God in the midst of things He knows good and well we cannot comprehend.

BETH MOORE

Faith is nothing more or less than actively trusting God.

CATHERINE MARSHALL

Faith never knows where it is being led, but it loves the One who is leading.

OSWALD CHAMBERS

Faith does not concern itself
with the entire journey.
One step is enough.

—

MRS. CHARLES E. COWMAN

A PRAYER FOR TODAY

Dear Lord, help me to be a woman of faith. Help me to remember that You are always near and that You can overcome any challenge. With Your love and Your power, Lord, I can live courageously and faithfully today and every day. Amen

YOUR THOUGHTS ABOUT FAITH

_____

_____

_____

_____

_____

_____

_____

_____

_____

_____

_____

_____

_____

_____

THE POWER OF
HIS PROMISES

Heaven and earth will pass away,
but My words will never pass away.

—

MATTHEW 24:35 HCSB

God's promises are found in a book like no other: the Holy Bible. The Bible is a roadmap for life here on earth and for life eternal. As Christians, we are called upon to trust its promises, to follow its commandments, and to share its Good News.

As believers, we must study the Bible each day and meditate upon its meaning for our lives. Otherwise, we deprive ourselves of a priceless gift from our Creator. God's Holy Word is, indeed, a transforming, life-changing, one-of-a-kind treasure. And, a passing acquaintance with the Good Book is insufficient for Christians who seek to obey God's Word and to understand His will.

God has made promises to mankind and to you. God's promises never fail and they never grow old. You must trust those promises and share them with your family, with your friends, and with the world.

A TIMELY TIP FROM THE GARDEN OF FAITH

Charles Swindoll writes, "There are four words I wish we would never forget, and they are, 'God keeps his word.'" And, when it comes to studying God's Word, school is always in session.

PROMISES FROM GOD'S WORD

But the word of the Lord endures forever. And this is the word that was preached as the gospel to you.

1 PETER 1:25 HCSB

All Scripture is inspired by God and is profitable for teaching, for rebuking, for correcting, for training in righteousness, so that the man of God may be complete, equipped for every good work.

2 TIMOTHY 3:16-17 HCSB

For the word of God is living and effective and sharper than any two-edged sword, penetrating as far as to divide soul, spirit, joints, and marrow; it is a judge of the ideas and thoughts of the heart.

HEBREWS 4:12 HCSB

The one who is from God listens to God's words. This is why you don't listen, because you are not from God.

JOHN 8:47 HCSB

Every word of God is pure; He is a shield to those who put their trust in Him.

PROVERBS 30:5 NKJV

MORE GREAT IDEAS

Words fail to express my love for this holy Book, my gratitude for its author, for His love and goodness. How shall I thank him for it?

LOTTIE MOON

Only through routine, regular exposure to God's Word can you and I draw out the nutrition needed to grow a heart of faith.

ELIZABETH GEORGE

The Bible became a living book and a guide for my life.

VONETTE BRIGHT

I need the spiritual revival that comes from spending quiet time alone with Jesus in prayer and in thoughtful meditation on His Word.

ANNE GRAHAM LOTZ

God can see clearly no matter how dark or foggy the night is. Trust His Word to guide you safely home.

LISA WHELCHEL

God's Word is a light not only to our path but also to our thinking. Place it in your heart today, and you will never walk in darkness.

JONI EARECKSON TADA

Walking in faith brings you to the Word of God. There you will be healed, cleansed, fed, nurtured, equipped, and matured.

KAY ARTHUR

If we are not continually fed with God's Word, we will starve spiritually.

STORMIE OMARTIAN

Daily Bible reading is essential to victorious living and real Christian growth.

BILLY GRAHAM

Jesus is Victor. Calvary is the place of victory. Obedience is the pathway of victory. Bible study and prayer is the preparation for victory.

CORRIE TEN BOOM

Weave the unveiling fabric of
God's word through your
heart and mind.
It will hold strong,
even if the rest of life unravels.

—

GIGI GRAHAM TCHIVIDJIAN

A PRAYER FOR TODAY

Dear Lord, Your scripture is a light unto the world; let me study it, trust it, and share it with all who cross my path. In all that I do, help me be a woman who is a worthy witness for You as I share the Good News of Your perfect Son and Your perfect Word. Amen

YOUR THOUGHTS ABOUT TRUSTING GOD'S PROMISES

_____

_____

_____

_____

_____

_____

_____

_____

_____

_____

_____

3

ENTRUSTING YOUR HOPES TO GOD

You, Lord, give true peace to those who depend on you, because they trust you.

—

ISAIAH 26:3 NCV

As every woman knows, hope is a perishable commodity. Despite God's promises, despite Christ's love, and despite our countless blessings, we frail human beings can still lose hope from time to time. When we do, we need the encouragement of Christian friends, the life-changing power of prayer, and the healing truth of God's Holy Word. If we find ourselves falling into the spiritual traps of worry and discouragement, we should seek the healing touch of Jesus and the encouraging words of fellow Christians. Even though this world can be a place of trials and struggles, God has promised us peace, joy, and eternal life if we give ourselves to Him.

A TIMELY TIP FROM THE GARDEN OF FAITH

If you're experiencing hard times, you'll be wise to start spending more time with God. And if you do your part, God will do His part. So never be afraid to hope—or to pray—for a miracle.

PROMISES FROM GOD'S WORD

Let us hold on to the confession of our hope without wavering, for He who promised is faithful.

HEBREWS 10:23 HCSB

For in You, O Lord, I hope; You will hear, O Lord my God.

PSALM 38:15 NKJV

The Lord is good to those who wait for Him, to the soul who seeks Him. It is good that one should hope and wait quietly for the salvation of the Lord.

LAMENTATIONS 3:25-26 NKJV

Now may the God of hope fill you with all joy and peace in believing, so that you may overflow with hope by the power of the Holy Spirit.

ROMANS 15:13 HCSB

Finally brothers, whatever is true, whatever is honorable, whatever is just, whatever is pure, whatever is lovely, whatever is commendable—if there is any moral excellence and if there is any praise—dwell on these things.

PHILIPPIANS 4:8 HCSB

MORE GREAT IDEAS

Never yield to gloomy anticipation. Place your hope and confidence in God. He has no record of failure.

MRS. CHARLES E. COWMAN

The best we can hope for in this life is a knothole peek at the shining realities ahead. Yet a glimpse is enough. It's enough to convince our hearts that whatever sufferings and sorrows currently assail us aren't worthy of comparison to that which waits over the horizon.

JONI EARECKSON TADA

I discovered that sorrow was not to be feared but rather endured with hope and expectancy that God would use it to visit and bless my life.

JILL BRISCOE

The future lies all before us. Shall it only be a slight advance upon what we usually do? Ought it not to be a bound, a leap forward to altitudes of endeavor and success undreamed of before?

ANNIE ARMSTRONG

Love is the seed of all hope. It is the enticement to trust, to risk, to try, and to go on.

GLORIA GAITHER

Easter comes each year to remind us of a truth that is eternal and universal. The empty tomb of Easter morning says to you and me, "Of course you'll encounter trouble. But behold a God of power who can take any evil and turn it into a door of hope."

CATHERINE MARSHALL

Always stay connected to people and seek out things that bring you joy. Dream with abandon. Pray confidently.

BARBARA JOHNSON

Waiting is the hardest kind of work, but God knows best, and we may joyfully leave all in His hands.

LOTTIE MOON

Remember always that there are two things which are more utterly incompatible even than oil and water, and these two are trust and worry.

HANNAH WHITALL SMITH

Hope looks for the good in people,
opens doors for people,
discovers what can be done
to help, lights a candle,
does not yield to cynicism.
Hope sets people free.

—

BARBARA JOHNSON

A PRAYER FOR TODAY

Dear Lord, I will place my hope in You. If I become discouraged, I will turn to You. If I am afraid, I will seek strength in You. In every aspect of my life, I will trust You. You are my Father, and I will place my hope, my trust, and my faith in You. Amen

YOUR THOUGHTS ABOUT THE POWER OF HOPE

_____

_____

_____

_____

_____

_____

_____

_____

_____

_____

_____

PEACE FOR
THE JOURNEY

Peace I leave with you, My peace I give to you;
not as the world gives do I give to you.
Let not your heart be troubled,
neither let it be afraid.

—

JOHN 14:27 NKJV

The beautiful words of John 14:27 give us hope: "Peace I leave with you, my peace I give unto you . . . ." Jesus offers us peace, not as the world gives, but as He alone gives. We, as believers, can accept His peace or ignore it.

When we accept the peace of Jesus Christ into our hearts, our lives are transformed. And then, because we possess the gift of peace, we can share that gift with fellow Christians, family members, and friends. If, on the other hand, we choose to ignore the gift of peace—for whatever reason—we cannot share what we do not possess.

As every woman knows, peace can be a scarce commodity in our demanding, tech-savvy world. How, then, can we find the peace that we so desperately desire? By turning our days and our lives over to God. Elisabeth Elliot writes, "If my life is surrendered to God, all is well. Let me not grab it back, as though it were in peril in His hand but would be safer in mine!" May we give our lives, our hopes, and our prayers to the Lord, and, by doing so, accept His will and His peace.

A TIMELY TIP FROM THE GARDEN OF FAITH

Peace starts at home. You have a big role to play in helping to maintain a peaceful home. It's a big job, so don't be afraid to ask for help . . . especially God's help.

PROMISES FROM GOD'S WORD

God has called us to peace.

1 CORINTHIANS 7:15 NKJV

Be of good comfort, be of one mind, live in peace; and the God of love and peace will be with you.

2 CORINTHIANS 13:11 NKJV

For He is our peace.

EPHESIANS 2:14 HCSB

The result of righteousness will be peace; the effect of righteousness will be quiet confidence forever.

ISAIAH 32:17 HCSB

Now the fruit of righteousness is sown in peace by those who make peace.

JAMES 3:18 NKJV

MORE GREAT IDEAS

When we do what is right, we have contentment, peace, and happiness.

BEVERLY LAHAYE

To know God as He really is—in His essential nature and character—is to arrive at a citadel of peace that circumstances may storm, but can never capture.

CATHERINE MARSHALL

I believe that in every time and place it is within our power to acquiesce in the will of God—and what peace it brings to do so!

ELISABETH ELLIOT

The fruit of our placing all things in God's hands is the presence of His abiding peace in our hearts.

HANNAH WHITALL SMITH

Prayer guards hearts and minds and causes God to bring peace out of chaos.

BETH MOORE

In the center of a hurricane there is absolute quiet and peace. There is no safer place than in the center of the will of God.

CORRIE TEN BOOM

What peace can they have who are not at peace with God?

MATTHEW HENRY

God is in control of history; it's His story. Doesn't that give you a great peace—especially when world events seems so tumultuous and insane?

KAY ARTHUR

The next time you're disappointed, don't panic. Don't give up. Just be patient and let God remind you he's still in control.

MAX LUCADO

The peace that Jesus gives is never engineered by circumstances on the outside.

OSWALD CHAMBERS

Peace does not mean to be
in a place where there is no noise,
trouble, or hard work.
Peace means to be in the midst
of all those things and still be
calm in your heart.

—

CATHERINE MARSHALL

A PRAYER FOR TODAY

Dear Lord, I will open my heart to You. And I thank You, God, for Your love, for Your peace, and for Your Son. Amen

YOUR THOUGHTS ABOUT GOD'S PEACE

_____

_____

_____

_____

_____

_____

_____

_____

_____

_____

_____

_____

_____

A JOYFUL SPIRIT

These things I have spoken to you,
that My joy may remain in you,
and that your joy may be full.

—

JOHN 15:11 NKJV

God's Word makes it clear: He intends that His joy should become our joy. The Lord intends that believers should share His love with His joy in their hearts. Yet sometimes, amid the inevitable hustle and bustle of life here on earth, we can forfeit—albeit temporarily—God's joy as we wrestle with the challenges of daily living.

Joni Eareckson Tada spoke for Christian women of every generation when she observed, "I wanted the deepest part of me to vibrate with that ancient yet familiar longing, that desire for something that would fill and overflow my soul."

Psalm 100 reminds us that, as believers, we have every reason to celebrate: "Shout for joy to the LORD, all the earth. Worship the LORD with gladness" (vv. 1-2 NIV). These words most certainly apply to you.

Are you a woman whose joy is clearly evident to your family and friends? If so, congratulations—you're doing God's will. But, if you find yourself feeling discouraged or worse, it's time to slow down and have a quiet conversation with your Creator.

If your heart is heavy, turn to Christ. He will give you peace and joy. And if you already have the joy of Christ in your heart, share it freely, just as Christ has freely shared His joy with you.

PROMISES FROM GOD'S WORD

Weeping may spend the night, but there is joy in the morning.
PSALM 30:5 HCSB

Rejoice in the Lord always. I will say it again: Rejoice!
PHILIPPIANS 4:4 HCSB

Make me to hear joy and gladness.

PSALM 51:8 KJV

*Now I am coming to You, and I speak these things in the world
so that they may have My joy completed in them.*
JOHN 17:13 HCSB

A TIMELY TIP FROM THE GARDEN OF FAITH

Joy begins with a choice—the choice to establish a genuine relationship with God and His Son. Joy does not depend upon your circumstances, but upon your relationship with God.

MORE GREAT IDEAS

If you're a thinking Christian, you will be a joyful Christian.

MARIE T. FREEMAN

There may be no trumpet sound or loud applause when we make a right decision, just a calm sense of resolution and peace.

GLORIA GAITHER

The Christian lifestyle is not one of legalistic do's and don'ts, but one that is positive, attractive, and joyful.

VONETTE BRIGHT

What is your focus today? Joy comes when it is Jesus first, others second...then you.

KAY ARTHUR

Jesus did not promise to change the circumstances around us. He promised great peace and pure joy to those who would learn to believe that God actually controls all things.

CORRIE TEN BOOM

Joy is a by-product not of happy circumstances, education or talent, but of a healthy relationship with God and a determination to love Him no matter what.

BARBARA JOHNSON

Unparalleled joy and victory come from allowing Christ to do "the hard thing" with us.

BETH MOORE

The time for universal praise is sure to come some day. Let us begin to do our part now.

HANNAH WHITALL SMITH

Jesus wants Life for us, Life with a capital L.

JOHN ELDREDGE

To a world that was spiritually dry and populated with parched lives scorched by sin, Jesus was the Living Water who would quench the thirsty soul, saving it from "bondage" and filling it with satisfaction and joy and purpose and meaning.

ANNE GRAHAM LOTZ

This is my story, this is my song,
praising my Savior all the day long;
this is my story, this is my song,
praising my Savior all the day long.

—

FANNY CROSBY

A PRAYER FOR TODAY

Dear Lord, You have given me so many blessings, starting with my family. I will keep joy in my heart as I thank You, Lord, for every single blessing You've given me. Amen

YOUR THOUGHTS ABOUT JOY

CHAPTER

6

EMBRACED BY GOD

For God so loved the world, that he gave his
only begotten Son, that whosoever believeth in him
should not perish, but have everlasting life.

—

JOHN 3:16 KJV

God's love for you is bigger and better than you can imagine. In fact, God's love is far too big to comprehend (in this lifetime). But this much you should know: God loves you so much that He sent His Son Jesus to come to this earth and to die for you. And, when you accepted Jesus into your heart, God gave you a gift that is more precious than gold: the gift of eternal life.

The words of Romans 8 make this promise: "For I am persuaded that neither death nor life, nor angels nor principalities nor powers, nor things present nor things to come, nor height nor depth, nor any other created thing, shall be able to separate us from the love of God which is in Christ Jesus our Lord" (vv. 38-39 NKJV).

Sometimes, in the crush of your daily duties, God may seem far away, but He is not. God is everywhere you have ever been and everywhere you will ever go. He is with you night and day; He knows your thoughts and He hears your prayers. When you earnestly seek Him, you will find Him because He is here, waiting patiently for you to reach out to Him.

Reach out to God today and always. Encourage your family members to do likewise. And then, arm-in-arm with your loved ones, praise God for blessings that are simply too numerous to count.

PROMISES FROM GOD'S WORD

For the Lord is good, and His love is eternal; His faithfulness endures through all generations.

PSALM 100:5 HCSB

[Because of] the Lord's faithful love we do not perish, for His mercies never end. They are new every morning; great is Your faithfulness!

LAMENTATIONS 3:22-23 HCSB

Help me, Lord my God; save me according to Your faithful love.

PSALM 109:26 HCSB

Whoever is wise will observe these things, and they will understand the lovingkindness of the Lord.

PSALM 107:43 NKJV

A TIMELY TIP FROM THE GARDEN OF FAITH

Remember: God's love for you is too big to understand with your brain . . . but it's not too big to feel with your heart?

MORE GREAT IDEAS

The fact is, God no longer deals with us in judgment but in mercy. If people got what they deserved, this old planet would have ripped apart at the seams centuries ago. Praise God that because of His great love "we are not consumed, for his compassions never fail" (Lam. 3:22).

JONI EARECKSON TADA

Being loved by Him whose opinion matters most gives us the security to risk loving, too—even loving ourselves.

GLORIA GAITHER

Snuggle in God's arms. When you are hurting, when you feel lonely or left out, let Him cradle you, comfort you, reassure you of His all-sufficient power and love.

KAY ARTHUR

God's love is measureless. It is more: it is boundless. It has no bounds because it is not a thing but a facet of the essential nature of God. His love is something he is, and because he is infinite, that love can enfold the whole created world in itself and have room for ten thousand times ten thousand worlds beside.

A. W. TOZER

Jesus loves us with fidelity, purity, constancy, and passion, no matter how imperfect we are.

STORMIE OMARTIAN

There is no pit so deep that God's love is not deeper still.

CORRIE TEN BOOM

Accepting God's love as a gift instead of trying to earn it had somehow seemed presumptuous and arrogant to me, when, in fact, my pride was tricking me into thinking that I could merit His love and forgiveness with my own strength.

LISA WHELCHEL

God is a God of unconditional, unremitting love, a love that corrects and chastens but never ceases.

KAY ARTHUR

God proved his love on the cross. When Christ hung, and bled, and died, it was God saying to the world—I love you.

BILLY GRAHAM

As God's children, we are
the recipients of lavish love—
a love that motivates us to keep
trusting even when we have
no idea what God is doing.

—

BETH MOORE

A PRAYER FOR TODAY

Lord, I know that You love me. I will accept Your love—and share it—today and every day. Amen

YOUR THOUGHTS ABOUT GOD'S LOVE

_____

_____

_____

_____

_____

_____

_____

_____

_____

_____

_____

_____

_____

HE RENEWS

*I will give you a new heart and
put a new spirit within you.*

—

EZEKIEL 36:26 HCSB

For busy women living in a fast-paced 21st-century world, life may seem like a merry-go-round that never stops turning. If that description seems to fit your life, then you may find yourself running short on patience, or strength, or both. If you're feeling tired or discouraged, there is a source from which you can draw the power needed to recharge your spiritual batteries. That source is God.

Are you exhausted or troubled? Turn your heart toward God in prayer. Are you weak or worried? Take the time—or, more accurately, make the time—to delve deeply into God's Holy Word. Are you spiritually depleted? Call upon fellow believers to support you, and call upon Christ to renew your spirit and your life. When you do, you'll discover that the Creator of the universe stands always ready and always able to create a new sense of wonderment and joy in you.

A TIMELY TIP FROM THE GARDEN OF FAITH

Do you need time for yourself? Take it. Ruth Bell Graham observed, "It is important that we take time out for ourselves—for relaxation, for refreshment." Enough said.

PROMISES FROM GOD'S WORD

But may the God of all grace, who called us to His eternal glory by Christ Jesus, after you have suffered a while, perfect, establish, strengthen, and settle you.

1 PETER 5:10 NKJV

Finally, brothers, rejoice. Be restored, be encouraged, be of the same mind, be at peace, and the God of love and peace will be with you.

2 CORINTHIANS 13:11 HCSB

But those who wait on the Lord shall renew their strength; they shall mount up with wings like eagles, they shall run and not be weary, they shall walk and not faint.

ISAIAH 40:31 NKJV

Therefore if anyone is in Christ, he is a new creature; the old things passed away; behold, new things have come.

2 CORINTHIANS 5:17 HCSB

Do not remember the former things, nor consider the things of old. Behold, I will do a new thing.

ISAIAH 43:18-19 NKJV

MORE GREAT IDEAS

God specializes in things fresh and firsthand. His plans for you this year may outshine those of the past. He's prepared to fill your days with reasons to give Him praise.

JONI EARECKSON TADA

Repentance removes old sins and wrong attitudes, and it opens the way for the Holy Spirit to restore our spiritual health.

SHIRLEY DOBSON

All the power of God—the same power that hung the stars in place and put the planets in their courses and transformed Earth—now resides in you to energize and strengthen you to become the person God created you to be.

ANNE GRAHAM LOTZ

Troubles we bear trustfully can bring us a fresh vision of God and a new outlook on life, an outlook of peace and hope.

BILLY GRAHAM

When we invite Jesus into our lives, we experience life in the fullest, most vital sense.

CATHERINE MARSHALL

How motivating it has been for me to view my early morning devotions as time of retreat alone with Jesus, Who desires that I "come with Him by myself to a quiet place" in order to pray, read His Word, listen for His voice, and be renewed in my spirit.

ANNE GRAHAM LOTZ

Jesus is calling the weary to rest, / Calling today, calling today, / Bring Him your burden and you shall be blest; / He will not turn you away.

FANNY CROSBY

Like a spring of pure water, God's peace in our hearts brings cleansing and refreshment to our minds and bodies.

BILLY GRAHAM

The same voice that brought Lazarus out of the tomb raised us to newness of life.

C. H. SPURGEON

He is the God of wholeness
and restoration.

—

STORMIE OMARTIAN

A PRAYER FOR TODAY

Lord, I am an imperfect woman. Because my faith is limited, I may become overwhelmed by the demands of the day. When I feel tired or discouraged, renew my strength. When I am worried, let me turn my thoughts and my prayers to You. Let me trust Your promises, Dear Lord, and let me accept Your unending love, now and forever. Amen

YOUR THOUGHTS ABOUT RENEWAL

YOUR JOURNEY WITH GOD

For it is God who is working among you both the willing and the working for His good purpose.

—

PHILIPPIANS 2:13 HCSB

"**W**hat on earth does God intend for me to do with my life?" It's an easy question to ask but, for many of us, a difficult question to answer. Why? Because God's purposes aren't always clear to us. Sometimes we wander aimlessly in a wilderness of our own making. And sometimes, we struggle mightily against God in an unsuccessful attempt to find success and happiness through our own means, not His.

If you're a woman who sincerely seeks God's guidance, He will give it. But, He will make His revelations known to you in a way and in a time of His choosing, not yours, so be patient. If you prayerfully petition God and work diligently to discern His intentions, He will, in time, lead you to a place of joyful abundance and eternal peace.

Sometimes, God's intentions will be clear to you; other times, God's plan will seem uncertain at best. But even on those difficult days when you are unsure which way to turn, you must never lose sight of these overriding facts: God created you for a reason; He has important work for you to do; and He's waiting patiently for you to do it.

A TIMELY TIP FROM THE GARDEN OF FAITH

God has a wonderful plan for your life. And the time to start looking for that plan—and living it—is now. (Psalm 16:11)

PROMISES FROM GOD'S WORD

We know that all things work together for the good of those who love God: those who are called according to His purpose.

ROMANS 8:28 HCSB

I will instruct you and show you the way to go; with My eye on you, I will give counsel.

PSALM 32:8 HCSB

You reveal the path of life to me; in Your presence is abundant joy; in Your right hand are eternal pleasures.

PSALM 16:11 HCSB

Commit your activities to the Lord and your plans will be achieved.

PROVERBS 16:3 HCSB

To everything there is a season, a time for every purpose under heaven.

ECCLESIASTES 3:1 NKJV

MORE GREAT IDEAS

It's incredible to realize that what we do each day has meaning in the big picture of God's plan.

BILL HYBELS

If you want purpose and meaning and satisfaction and fulfillment and peace and hope and joy and abundant life that lasts forever, look to Jesus.

ANNE GRAHAM LOTZ

How much of our lives are, well, so daily. How often our hours are filled with the mundane, seemingly unimportant things that have to be done, whether at home or work. These very "daily" tasks could become a celebration of praise. "It is through consecration," someone has said, "that drudgery is made divine."

GIGI GRAHAM TCHIVIDJIAN

Great relief and satisfaction can come from seeking God's priorities for us in each season, discerning what is "best" in the midst of many noble opportunities, and pouring our most excellent energies into those things.

BETH MOORE

His life is our light—our purpose and meaning and reason for living.

ANNE GRAHAM LOTZ

Yesterday is just experience but tomorrow is glistening with purpose—and today is the channel leading from one to the other.

BARBARA JOHNSON

In the very place where God has put us, whatever its limitations, whatever kind of work it may be, we may indeed serve the Lord Christ.

ELISABETH ELLIOT

God specializes in things fresh and firsthand. His plans for you this year may outshine those of the past. He's prepared to fill your days with reasons to give Him praise.

JONI EARECKSON TADA

Whether you have twenty years left, ten years, one year, one month, one day, or just one hour, there is something very important God wants you to do that can add to His kingdom and your blessing.

BILL BRIGHT

Only God's chosen task for you
will ultimately satisfy.
Do not wait until it is too late
to realize the privilege of
serving Him in His chosen
position for you.

—

BETH MOORE

A PRAYER FOR TODAY

Lord, You've got something You want me to do—help me to figure out exactly what it is. Give me Your blessings and lead me along a path that is pleasing to You . . . today, tomorrow, and forever. Amen

YOUR THOUGHTS ABOUT FINDING PURPOSE

_____

_____

_____

_____

_____

_____

_____

_____

_____

_____

_____

_____

FORGIVENESS NOW

*And whenever you stand praying,
if you have anything against anyone, forgive him,
so that your Father in heaven may also
forgive you your wrongdoing.*

—

MARK 11:25 HCSB

Even the most mild-mannered women will, on occasion, have reason to become angry with the inevitable shortcomings of family members and friends. But wise women are quick to forgive others, just as God has forgiven them.

The commandment to forgive others is clearly a part of God's Word, but oh how difficult a commandment it can be to follow. Because we are imperfect beings, we are quick to anger, quick to blame, slow to forgive, and even slower to forget. No matter. Even when forgiveness is difficult, God's instructions are straightforward: As Christians who have received the gift of forgiveness, we must now share that gift with others.

If, in your heart, you hold bitterness against even a single person, forgive. If there exists even one person, alive or dead, whom you have not forgiven, follow God's commandment and His will for your life: forgive. If you are embittered against yourself for some past mistake or shortcoming, forgive. Then, to the best of your abilities, forget, and move on. Bitterness and regret are not part of God's plan for your life. Forgiveness is. And once you've forgiven others, you can then turn your thoughts to a far more pleasant subject: the incredibly bright future that God has promised.

PROMISES FROM GOD'S WORD

Be merciful, just as your Father also is merciful.

LUKE 6:36 HCSB

Then Peter came to Him and said, "Lord, how many times could my brother sin against me and I forgive him? As many as seven times?" "I tell you, not as many as seven," Jesus said to him, "but 70 times seven."

MATTHEW 18:21-22 HCSB

You have heard that it was said, You shall love your neighbor and hate your enemy. But I tell you, love your enemies, and pray for those who persecute you, so that you may be sons of your Father in heaven.

MATTHEW 5:43-45 HCSB

A TIMELY TIP FROM THE GARDEN OF FAITH

Face facts: forgiving can be a very hard thing to do. No matter. God instructs us to forgive others (and to keep forgiving them), period.

MORE GREAT IDEAS

How often should you forgive the other person? Only as many times as you want God to forgive you!

MARIE T. FREEMAN

Forgiveness is actually the best revenge because it not only sets us free from the person we forgive, but it frees us to move into all that God has in store for us.

STORMIE OMARTIAN

To be a Christian means to forgive the inexcusable, because God has forgiven the inexcusable in you.

C. S. LEWIS

God expects us to forgive others as He has forgiven us; we are to follow His example by having a forgiving heart.

VONETTE BRIGHT

Forgiveness is the key that unlocks the door of resentment and the handcuffs of hate. It is a power that breaks the chains of bitterness and the shackles of selfishness.

CORRIE TEN BOOM

I believe that forgiveness can become a continuing cycle: because God forgives us, we're to forgive others; because we forgive others, God forgives us. Scripture presents both parts of the cycle.

SHIRLEY DOBSON

Jesus had a forgiving and understanding heart. If he lives within us, mercy will temper our relationships with our fellow men.

BILLY GRAHAM

Forgiveness is contagious. First you forgive them, and pretty soon, they'll forgive you, too.

MARIE T. FREEMAN

There is no use in talking as if forgiveness were easy. I could say of a certain man, "Have I forgiven him more times than I can count?" For we find that the work of forgiveness has to be done over and over again.

C. S. LEWIS

Sometimes, we need a housecleaning of the heart.

CATHERINE MARSHALL

Grudges are like hand grenades;
it is wise to release them
before they destroy you.

—

BARBARA JOHNSON

A PRAYER FOR TODAY

Dear Lord, let forgiveness rule my heart, even when forgiveness is difficult. Let me be Your obedient servant, Lord, and let me be a woman who forgives others just as You have forgiven me. Amen

YOUR THOUGHTS ABOUT FORGIVENESS

_____

_____

_____

_____

_____

_____

_____

_____

_____

_____

_____

_____

_____

TRUST HIM

Trust in the Lord with all your heart,
and do not rely on your own understanding;
think about Him in all your ways,
and He will guide you on the right paths.

—

PROVERBS 3:5-6 HCSB

W hen our dreams come true and our plans prove successful, we find it easy to thank our Creator and easy to trust His divine providence. But in times of sorrow or hardship, we may find ourselves questioning God's plans for our lives.

On occasion, you will confront circumstances that trouble you to the very core of your soul. It is during these difficult days that you must find the wisdom and the courage to trust your Heavenly Father despite your circumstances.

Are you a woman who seeks God's blessings for yourself and your family? Then trust Him. Trust Him with your relationships. Trust Him with your priorities. Follow His commandments and pray for His guidance. Trust Your Heavenly Father day by day, moment by moment—in good times and in trying times. Then, wait patiently for God's revelations . . . and prepare yourself for the abundance and peace that will most certainly be yours when you do.

A TIMELY TIP FROM THE GARDEN OF FAITH

One of the most important lessons that you can ever learn is to trust God for everything, and that includes timing. In other words, you should trust God to decide the best time for things to happen. Sometimes it's hard to trust God, but it's always the right thing to do.

PROMISES FROM GOD'S WORD

For the eyes of the Lord range throughout the earth to show Himself strong for those whose hearts are completely His.

2 CHRONICLES 16:9 HCSB

He granted their request because they trusted in Him.

1 CHRONICLES 5:20 HCSB

Let us hold fast the confession of our hope without wavering, for He who promised is faithful.

HEBREWS 10:23 NKJV

The one who understands a matter finds success, and the one who trusts in the Lord will be happy.

PROVERBS 16:20 HCSB

I know whom I have believed and am persuaded that He is able to guard what has been entrusted to me until that day.

2 TIMOTHY 1:12 HCSB

MORE GREAT IDEAS

Sometimes the very essence of faith is trusting God in the midst of things He knows good and well we cannot comprehend.

BETH MOORE

Are you serious about wanting God's guidance to become the person he wants you to be? The first step is to tell God that you know you can't manage your own life; that you need his help.

CATHERINE MARSHALL

Brother, is your faith looking upward today? / Trust in the promise of the Savior. / Sister, is the light shining bright on your way? / Trust in the promise of thy Lord.

FANNY CROSBY

Do not be afraid, then, that if you trust, or tell others to trust, the matter will end there. Trust is only the beginning and the continual foundation. When we trust Him, the Lord works, and His work is the important part of the whole matter.

HANNAH WHITALL SMITH

As God's children, we are the recipients of lavish love—a love that motivates us to keep trusting even when we have no idea what God is doing.

BETH MOORE

Victory is the result of Christ's life lived out in the believer. It is important to see that victory, not defeat, is God's purpose for His children.

CORRIE TEN BOOM

Once we recognize our need for Jesus, then the building of our faith begins. It is a daily, moment-by-moment life of absolute dependence upon Him for everything.

CATHERINE MARSHALL

Trusting God completely means having faith that he knows what is best for your life. You expect him to keep his promises, help you with problems, and do the impossible when necessary.

RICK WARREN

God is God. He knows what he is doing. When you can't trace his hand, trust his heart.

MAX LUCADO

Never be afraid to trust
an unknown future
to a known God.

—

CORRIE TEN BOOM

A PRAYER FOR TODAY

Dear Lord, as I take the next steps on my life's journey, let me take them with You. Whatever the coming day may bring, I will thank You for the opportunity to live abundantly. I will be Your faith-filled servant, Lord—and I will trust You—this day and forever. Amen

YOUR THOUGHTS ABOUT TRUSTING GOD

THE POWER OF PATIENCE

Rejoice in hope; be patient in affliction;
be persistent in prayer.

—

ROMANS 12:12 HCSB

Psalm 37:7 commands us to wait patiently for God. But as busy women in a fast-paced world, many of us find that waiting quietly for God is difficult. Why? Because we are fallible human beings seeking to live according to our own timetables, not God's. In our better moments, we realize that patience is not only a virtue, but it is also a commandment from God.

We human beings are impatient by nature. We know what we want, and we know exactly when we want it: NOW! But, God knows better. He has created a world that unfolds according to His plans, not our own. As believers, we must trust His wisdom and His goodness.

God instructs us to be patient in all things. We must be patient with our families, our friends, and our associates. We must also be patient with our Creator as He unfolds His plan for our lives. And that's as it should be. After all, think about how patient God has been with us.

A TIMELY TIP FROM THE GARDEN OF FAITH

God asks you to be a positive example to your family, to your friends, and to the world. The rest is up to you.

PROMISES FROM GOD'S WORD

Love is patient; love is kind.

1 CORINTHIANS 13:4 HCSB

A patient spirit is better than a proud spirit.

ECCLESIASTES 7:8 HCSB

Therefore the Lord is waiting to show you mercy, and is rising up to show you compassion, for the Lord is a just God. Happy are all who wait patiently for Him.

ISAIAH 30:18 HCSB

Be gentle to everyone, able to teach, and patient.

2 TIMOTHY 2:23 HCSB

My brethren, count it all joy when you fall into various trials, knowing that the testing of your faith produces patience. But let patience have its perfect work, that you may be perfect and complete, lacking nothing.

JAMES 1:2-4 NKJV

MORE GREAT IDEAS

How do you wait upon the Lord? First you must learn to sit at His feet and take time to listen to His words.

KAY ARTHUR

Waiting is the hardest kind of work, but God knows best, and we may joyfully leave all in His hands.

LOTTIE MOON

Let me encourage you to continue to wait with faith. God may not perform a miracle, but He is trustworthy to touch you and make you whole where there used to be a hole.

LISA WHELCHEL

Waiting is an essential part of spiritual discipline. It can be the ultimate test of faith.

ANNE GRAHAM LOTZ

If God is diligent, surely we ought to be diligent in doing our duty to Him. Think how patient and diligent God has been to us!

OSWALD CHAMBERS

When we read of the great Biblical leaders, we see that it was not uncommon for God to ask them to wait, not just a day or two, but for years, until God was ready for them to act.

GLORIA GAITHER

You can't step in front of God and not get in trouble. When He says, "Go three steps," don't go four.

CHARLES STANLEY

God is more patient with us than we are with ourselves.

MAX LUCADO

Those who have had to wait and work for happiness seem to enjoy it more, because they never take it for granted.

BARBARA JOHNSON

If you want to hear God's voice clearly and you are uncertain, then remain in His presence until He changes that uncertainty. Often much can happen during this waiting for the Lord. Sometimes He changes pride into humility; doubt into faith and peace.

CORRIE TEN BOOM

We must learn to wait.
There is grace supplied
to the one who waits.

—

MRS. CHARLES E. COWMAN

A PRAYER FOR TODAY

Lord, give me patience. When I am hurried, give me peace. When I am frustrated, give me perspective. When I am angry, let me turn my heart to You. Today, let me become a more patient woman, Dear Lord, as I trust in You and in Your master plan for my life. Amen

YOUR THOUGHTS ABOUT WAYS
TO BE MORE PATIENT

_____

_____

_____

_____

_____

_____

_____

_____

_____

_____

CONTINUING TO GROW

*For this reason also, since the day we heard this,
we haven't stopped praying for you.
We are asking that you may be filled with
the knowledge of His will in all wisdom and
spiritual understanding.*

—

COLOSSIANS 1:9 HCSB

When will you be a "fully-grown" Christian woman? Hopefully never—or at least not until you arrive in heaven! As a believer living here on planet earth, you're never "fully grown"; you always have the potential to keep growing.

Many of life's most important lessons are painful to learn, but spiritual growth need not take place only in times of pain and hardship. Whatever your circumstances, God is always standing at the door; whenever you are ready to reach out to Him, He will answer.

In those quiet moments when you open your heart to God, the One who made you keeps remaking you. He gives you direction, perspective, wisdom, and courage. And, the appropriate moment to accept those spiritual gifts is always the present one.

Would you like a time-tested formula for spiritual growth? Here it is: keep studying God's Word, keep obeying His commandments, keep praying (and listening for answers), and seek to live in the center of God's will. When you do, you will never be a "stagnant" believer. You will, instead, be a growing Christian . . . and that's precisely the kind of Christian God wants you to be.

A TIMELY TIP FROM THE GARDEN OF FAITH

Spiritual maturity is a journey, not a destination. A growing relationship with God should be your highest priority.

PROMISES FROM GOD'S WORD

But grow in the grace and knowledge of our Lord and Savior Jesus Christ. To Him be the glory both now and to the day of eternity.

2 PETER 3:18 HCSB

Therefore, leaving the elementary message about the Messiah, let us go on to maturity.

HEBREWS 6:1 HCSB

For You, O God, have tested us; You have refined us as silver is refined. You brought us into the net; You laid affliction on our backs. You have caused men to ride over our heads; we went through fire and through water; but You brought us out to rich fulfillment.

PSALM 66:10–12 NKJV

For though by this time you ought to be teachers, you need someone to teach you again the basic principles of God's revelation. You need milk, not solid food. Now everyone who lives on milk is inexperienced with the message about righteousness, because he is an infant. But solid food is for the mature—for those whose senses have been trained to distinguish between good and evil.

HEBREWS 5:12-14 HCSB

MORE GREAT IDEAS

We set our eyes on the finish line, forgetting the past, and straining toward the mark of spiritual maturity and fruitfulness.

VONETTE BRIGHT

You cannot be the person God meant you to be, and you cannot live the life he meant you to live, unless you live from the heart.

JOHN ELDREDGE

Aim at Heaven and you will get earth "thrown in"; aim at earth and you will get neither.

C. S. LEWIS

If all struggles and sufferings were eliminated, the spirit would no more reach maturity than would the child.

ELISABETH ELLIOT

Grow, dear friends, but grow, I beseech you, in God's way, which is the only true way.

HANNAH WHITALL SMITH

Growth in depth and strength and consistency and fruitfulness and ultimately in Christlikeness is only possible when the winds of life are contrary to personal comfort.

ANNE GRAHAM LOTZ

You are either becoming more like Christ every day or you're becoming less like Him. There is no neutral position in the Lord.

STORMIE OMARTIAN

God is teaching me to become more and more "teachable": To keep evolving. To keep taking the risk of learning something new . . . or unlearning something old and off base.

BETH MOORE

He makes us wait. He keeps us in the dark on purpose. He makes us walk when we want to run, sit still when we want to walk, for he has things to do in our souls that we are not interested in.

ELISABETH ELLIOT

There is wonderful freedom
and joy in coming to recognize
that the fun is in the becoming.

—

GLORIA GAITHER

A PRAYER FOR TODAY

Lord, help me to keep growing spiritually and emotionally. Let me live according to Your Word, and let me grow in my faith every day that I live. Amen

❧

YOUR THOUGHTS ABOUT SPIRITUAL GROWTH

_____

_____

_____

_____

_____

_____

_____

_____

_____

_____

_____

_____

BE STILL MY SOUL

Be still, and know that I am God . . . .

—

PSALM 46:10 KJV

Are you so busy that you rush through the day with scarcely a single moment for quiet contemplation and prayer? If so, it's time to reorder your priorities.

We live in a noisy world, a world filled with distractions, frustrations, and complications. But if we allow the distractions of a clamorous world to separate us from God's peace, we do ourselves a profound disservice. If we are to maintain righteous minds and compassionate hearts, we must take time each day for prayer and for meditation. We must make ourselves still in the presence of our Creator. We must quiet our minds and our hearts so that we might sense God's will, God's love, and God's Son.

Has the busy pace of life robbed you of the peace that might otherwise be yours through Jesus Christ? Nothing is more important than the time you spend with your Savior. So be still and claim the inner peace that is your spiritual birthright: the peace of Jesus Christ. It is offered freely; it has been paid for in full; it is yours for the asking.

PROMISES FROM GOD'S WORD

Be silent before Me.

ISAIAH 41:1 HCSB

Be silent before the Lord and wait expectantly for Him.

PSALM 37:7 HCSB

Truly my soul silently waits for God; from Him comes my salvation.

PSALM 62:1 NKJV

My soul, wait silently for God alone, for my expectation is from Him.

PSALM 62:5 NKJV

A TIMELY TIP FROM THE GARDEN OF FAITH

Try this: The next time you're driving alone, turn off the radio and cell phones. Then, have a quiet talk with God about His plans for your life. You may be surprised to discover that sometimes the most important answers are the ones you receive in silence.

MORE GREAT IDEAS

When we are in the presence of God, removed from distractions, we are able to hear him more clearly, and a secure environment has been established for the young and broken places in our hearts to surface.

JOHN ELDREDGE

Because Jesus Christ is our Great High Priest, not only can we approach God without a human "go-between," we can also hear and learn from God in some sacred moments without one.

BETH MOORE

Instead of waiting for the feeling, wait upon God. You can do this by growing still and quiet, then expressing in prayer what your mind knows is true about Him, even if your heart doesn't feel it at this moment.

SHIRLEY DOBSON

It is in that stillness that the Voice will be heard, the only voice in all the universe that speaks peace to the deepest part of us.

ELISABETH ELLIOT

Quiet time is giving God your undivided attention for a predetermined amount of time for the purpose of talking to and hearing from Him.

CHARLES STANLEY

I need the spiritual revival that comes from spending quiet time alone with Jesus in prayer and in thoughtful meditation on His Word.

ANNE GRAHAM LOTZ

In the center of a hurricane there is absolute quiet and peace. There is no safer place than in the center of the will of God.

CORRIE TEN BOOM

When we are in the presence of God, removed from distractions, we are able to hear him more clearly, and a secure environment has been established for the young and broken places in our hearts to surface.

JOHN ELDREDGE

Be quiet enough to hear God's whisper.

ANONYMOUS

The world is full of noise.
Might we not set ourselves to
learn silence, stillness, solitude?

—

ELISABETH ELLIOT

A PRAYER FOR TODAY

Dear Lord, let me be still before You. When I am hurried or distracted, slow me down and redirect my thoughts. When I am confused, give me perspective. Keep me mindful, Father, that You are always with me. And let me sense Your presence today, tomorrow, and forever. Amen

YOUR THOUGHTS ABOUT THE NEED TO SPEND QUIET TIME WITH GOD

CHAPTER

14

STRENGTH
FOR THE JOURNEY

And He said to me,
"My grace is sufficient for you,
for My strength is made perfect in weakness."

—

2 CORINTHIANS 12:9 NKJV

Where do you go to find strength? The gym? The health food store? The coffee shop down the street? There's a better source of strength, of course, and that source is God. He is a never-ending source of strength and courage if you call upon Him.

Are you an energized Christian? You should be. But if you're not, you must seek strength and renewal from the source that will never fail: that source, of course, is your Heavenly Father. And rest assured—when you sincerely petition Him, He will give you all the strength you need to live victoriously for Him.

Have you "tapped in" to the power of God? Have you turned your life and your heart over to Him, or are you muddling along under your own power? The answer to this question will determine the quality of your life here on earth and the destiny of your life throughout all eternity. So start tapping in—and remember that when it comes to strength, God is the Ultimate Source.

A TIMELY TIP FROM THE GARDEN OF FAITH

Feeling exhausted? Try this: Start getting more sleep each night; begin a program of regular, sensible exercise; avoid harmful food and drink; and turn your problems over to God . . . and the greatest of these is "turn your problems over to God."

PROMISES FROM GOD'S WORD

You, therefore, my child, be strong in the grace that is in Christ Jesus.

2 TIMOTHY 2:1 HCSB

The Lord is my strength and my song; He has become my salvation.

EXODUS 15:2 HCSB

He gives strength to the weary and strengthens the powerless.

ISAIAH 40:29 HCSB

But those who wait on the Lord shall renew their strength; they shall mount up with wings like eagles, they shall run and not be weary, they shall walk and not faint.

ISAIAH 40:31 NKJV

Finally, be strengthened by the Lord and by His vast strength.

EPHESIANS 6:10 HCSB

MORE GREAT IDEAS

Worry does not empty tomorrow of its sorrow; it empties today of its strength.

CORRIE TEN BOOM

One reason so much American Christianity is a mile wide and an inch deep is that Christians are simply tired. Sometimes you need to kick back and rest for Jesus' sake.

DENNIS SWANBERG

God does not dispense strength and encouragement like a druggist fills your prescription. The Lord doesn't promise to give us something to take so we can handle our weary moments. He promises us Himself. That is all. And that is enough.

CHARLES SWINDOLL

When you and I are related to Jesus Christ, our strength and wisdom and peace and joy and love and hope may run out, but His life rushes in to keep us filled to the brim. We are showered with blessings, not because of anything we have or have not done, but simply because of Him.

ANNE GRAHAM LOTZ

Sometimes I think spiritual and physical strength is like manna: you get just what you need for the day, no more.

SUZANNE DALE EZELL

We are never stronger than the moment we admit we are weak.

BETH MOORE

A divine strength is given to those who yield themselves to the Father and obey what He tells them to do.

WARREN WIERSBE

The amount of power you experience to live a victorious, triumphant Christian life is directly proportional to the freedom you give the Spirit to be Lord of your life!

ANNE GRAHAM LOTZ

When the dream of our heart is one that God has planted there, a strange happiness flows into us. At that moment, all of the spiritual resources of the universe are released to help us. Our praying is then at one with the will of God and becomes a channel for the Creator's purposes for us and our world.

CATHERINE MARSHALL

Hope can give us life.
It can provide energy that
would otherwise do us in
completely if we tried to
operate in our own strength.

—

BARBARA JOHNSON

A PRAYER FOR TODAY

Dear Heavenly Father, You are my strength and my protector. When I am troubled, You comfort me. When I am discouraged, You lift me up. When I am afraid, You deliver me. Let me turn to You, Lord, when I am weak. In times of adversity, let me trust Your plan, Lord, and whatever my circumstances, let me look to You for my strength and my salvation. Amen

YOUR THOUGHTS ABOUT
FINDING STRENGTH

_____

_____

_____

_____

_____

_____

_____

_____

_____

THANKSGIVING NOW

In everything give thanks;
for this is the will of God in Christ Jesus for you.

—

1 THESSALONIANS 5:18 NKJV

As busy women caught up in the inevitable demands of everyday life, we sometimes fail to pause and thank our Creator for the countless blessings He has bestowed upon us. And that's unfortunate because, as believing Christians, we are blessed beyond measure.

God sent His only Son to die for our sins. And, God has given us the priceless gifts of eternal love and eternal life. We, in turn, are instructed to approach our Heavenly Father with reverence and thanksgiving.

When we slow down and express our gratitude to the One who made us, we enrich our own lives and the lives of those around us. Thanksgiving should become a habit, a regular part of our daily routines. Yes, God has blessed us beyond measure, and we owe Him everything, including our eternal praise.

A TIMELY TIP FROM THE GARDEN OF FAITH

When is the best time to say "thanks" to God? Any time. God never takes a vacation, and He's always ready to hear from you. So what are you waiting for? You owe God everything . . . including your thanks.

PROMISES FROM GOD'S WORD

Thanks be to God for His indescribable gift.

2 CORINTHIANS 9:15 HCSB

Therefore as you have received Christ Jesus the Lord, walk in Him, rooted and built up in Him and established in the faith, just as you were taught, and overflowing with thankfulness.

COLOSSIANS 2:6-7 HCSB

Enter into His gates with thanksgiving, and into His courts with praise. Be thankful to Him, and bless His name. For the Lord is good; His mercy is everlasting, and His truth endures to all generations.

PSALM 100:4-5 NKJV

And whatever you do, in word or in deed, do everything in the name of the Lord Jesus, giving thanks to God the Father through Him.

COLOSSIANS 3:17 HCSB

Give thanks to the Lord, for He is good; His faithful love endures forever.

PSALM 106:1 HCSB

MORE GREAT IDEAS

Thanksgiving is good but Thanksliving is better.

JIM GALLERY

Thanksgiving or complaining—these words express two contrastive attitudes of the souls of God's children in regard to His dealings with them. The soul that gives thanks can find comfort in everything; the soul that complains can find comfort in nothing.

HANNAH WHITALL SMITH

The act of thanksgiving is a demonstration of the fact that you are going to trust and believe God.

KAY ARTHUR

God is worthy of our praise and is pleased when we come before Him with thanksgiving.

SHIRLEY DOBSON

It is only with gratitude that life becomes rich.

DIETRICH BONHOEFFER

Do you know that if at birth I had been able to make one petition, it would have been that I should be born blind? Because, when I get to heaven, the first face that shall ever gladden my sight will be that of my Savior!

FANNY CROSBY

Our ultimate aim in life is not to be healthy, wealthy, prosperous, or problem free. Our ultimate aim in life is to bring glory to God.

ANNE GRAHAM LOTZ

Words fail to express my love for this holy Book, my gratitude for its author, for His love and goodness. How shall I thank him for it?

LOTTIE MOON

If you pause to think—you'll have cause to thank!

ANONYMOUS

Every believer may be brought to understand that the only object of his life is to help to make Christ King on the earth.

ANDREW MURRAY

It is always possible to be
thankful for what is given
rather than to complain
about what is not given.
One or the other becomes
a habit of life.

—

ELISABETH ELLIOT

A PRAYER FOR TODAY

Dear Lord, I'm really thankful for all the good things I have. Today I will show You how grateful I am, not only by the words that I speak, but also by the way that I act. Amen

YOUR THOUGHTS ABOUT THINGS
TO BE THANKFUL FOR

THE GREATEST OF THESE . . .

Now these three remain: faith, hope, and love.
But the greatest of these is love.

—

1 CORINTHIANS 13:13 HCSB

As a woman, you know the profound love that you hold in your heart for your own family and friends. As a child of God, you can only imagine the infinite love that your Heavenly Father holds for you.

God made you in His own image and gave you salvation through the person of His Son Jesus Christ. And now, precisely because you are a wondrous creation treasured by God, a question presents itself: What will you do in response to the Creator's love? Will you ignore it or embrace it? Will you return it or neglect it? That decision, of course, is yours and yours alone.

When you embrace God's love, your life's purpose is forever changed. When you embrace God's love, you feel differently about yourself, your neighbors, your family, and your world. More importantly, you share God's message—and His love—with others.

Your Heavenly Father—a God of infinite love and mercy—is waiting to embrace you with open arms. Accept His love today and forever.

A TIMELY TIP FROM THE GARDEN OF FAITH

Be creative. There are many ways to say, "I love you." Find them. Use them. And keep using them.

PROMISES FROM GOD'S WORD

I pray that you, being rooted and firmly established in love, may be able to comprehend with all the saints what is the breadth and width, height and depth, and to know the Messiah's love that surpasses knowledge, so you may be filled with all the fullness of God.

EPHESIANS 3:17-19 HCSB

If I speak the languages of men and of angels, but do not have love, I am a sounding gong or a clanging cymbal.

1 CORINTHIANS 13:1 HCSB

Dear friends, if God loved us in this way, we also must love one another.

1 JOHN 4:11 HCSB

We love because He first loved us.

1 JOHN 4:19 HCSB

Above all, keep your love for one another at full strength, since love covers a multitude of sins.

1 PETER 4:8 HCSB

116

MORE GREAT IDEAS

Love is not soft as water is; it is solid as a rock on which the waves of hatred beat in vain.

CORRIE TEN BOOM

Love always means sacrifice.

ELISABETH ELLIOT

Line by line, moment by moment, special times are etched into our memories in the permanent ink of everlasting love in our relationships.

GLORIA GAITHER

Homes that are built on anything other than love are bound to crumble.

BILLY GRAHAM

Prayer is the ultimate love language. It communicates in ways we can't.

STORMIE OMARTIAN

Agape is a kind of love God demonstrates to one person through another.

BETH MOORE

Forgiveness is the precondition of love.

CATHERINE MARSHALL

Our Lord does not care so much for the importance of our works as for the love with which they are done.

ST. TERESA OF AVILA

He who is filled with love is filled with God Himself.

ST. AUGUSTINE

Love is extravagant in the price it is willing to pay, the time it is willing to give, the hardships it is willing to endure, and the strength it is willing to spend. Love never thinks in terms of "how little," but always in terms of "how much." Love gives, love knows, and love lasts.

JONI EARECKSON TADA

Love is the seed of all hope.
It is the enticement to trust,
to risk, to try, and to go on.

GLORIA GAITHER

A PRAYER FOR TODAY

Dear God, let me share Your love with the world. Make me a woman of compassion. Help me to recognize the needs of others. Let me forgive those who have hurt me, just as You have forgiven me. And let the love of Your Son shine in me and through me today, tomorrow, and throughout all eternity. Amen

YOUR THOUGHTS ABOUT LOVE

SENSING
GOD'S PRESENCE

*Draw near to God,
and He will draw near to you.*

—

JAMES 4:8 HCSB

Since God is everywhere, we are free to sense His presence whenever we take the time to quiet our souls and turn our prayers to Him. But sometimes, amid the incessant demands of everyday life, we turn our thoughts far from God; when we do, we suffer.

Do you set aside quiet moments each day to offer praise to your Creator? As a woman who has received the gift of God's grace, you most certainly should. Silence is a gift that you give to yourself and to God. During these moments of stillness, you will often sense the infinite love and power of your Creator—and He, in turn, will speak directly to your heart.

The familiar words of Psalm 46:10 remind us to "Be still, and know that I am God." When we do so, we encounter the awesome presence of our loving Heavenly Father, and we are comforted in the knowledge that God is not just near. He is here.

A TIMELY TIP FROM THE GARDEN OF FAITH

If you're here, God is here. If you're there, God is, too. You can't get away from Him or His love . . . thank goodness!

PROMISES FROM GOD'S WORD

You will seek Me and find Me when you search for Me with all your heart.

JEREMIAH 29:13 HCSB

The Lord is near all who call out to Him, all who call out to Him with integrity. He fulfills the desires of those who fear Him; He hears their cry for help and saves them.

PSALM 145:18-19 HCSB

Surely goodness and mercy shall follow me all the days of my life: and I will dwell in the house of the Lord for ever.

PSALM 23:6 KJV

I am not alone, because the Father is with Me.

JOHN 16:32 HCSB

I have set the Lord always before me; because He is at my right hand I shall not be moved.

PSALM 16:8 NKJV

MORE GREAT IDEAS

If you want to hear God's voice clearly and you are uncertain, then remain in His presence until He changes that uncertainty. Often, much can happen during this waiting for the Lord. Sometimes, he changes pride into humility, doubt into faith and peace.

CORRIE TEN BOOM

Give yourself a gift today: be present with yourself. God is. Enjoy your own personality. God does.

BARBARA JOHNSON

Through the death and broken body of Jesus Christ on the Cross, you and I have been given access to the presence of God when we approach Him by faith in prayer.

ANNE GRAHAM LOTZ

Our souls were made to live in an upper atmosphere, and we stifle and choke if we live on any lower level. Our eyes were made to look off from these heavenly heights, and our vision is distorted by any lower gazing.

HANNAH WHITALL SMITH

If your heart has grown cold, it is because you have moved away from the fire of His presence.

BETH MOORE

It is God to whom and with whom we travel, and while He is the End of our journey, He is also at every stopping place.

ELISABETH ELLIOT

Oh! what a Savior, gracious to all, / Oh! how His blessings round us fall, / Gently to comfort, kindly to cheer, / Sleeping or waking, God is near.

FANNY CROSBY

As I wander from village to village, I feel it is no idle fancy that the Master walks beside me and I hear his voice saying gently, "I am with you always, even unto the end."

LOTTIE MOON

The next time you hear a baby laugh or see an ocean wave, take note. Pause and listen as his Majesty whispers ever so gently, "I'm here."

MAX LUCADO

God is always near,
but the more I prayed,
the more this truth struck home.

—

ELIZABETH GEORGE

A PRAYER FOR TODAY

Dear Lord, You are always with me. Thank You for never leaving my side, even for a moment! Amen

∽

YOUR THOUGHTS ABOUT GOD'S PRESENCE

_____

_____

_____

_____

_____

_____

_____

_____

_____

_____

_____

_____

_____

THIS IS THE DAY

This is the day the LORD has made;
we will rejoice and be glad in it.

—

PSALM 118:24 NKJV

The words of Psalm 118:24 remind us of a profound yet simple truth: God created this day, and it's up to each of us to rejoice and to be grateful.

For Christian believers, every day begins and ends with God and His Son. Christ came to this earth to give us abundant life and eternal salvation. We give thanks to our Maker when we treasure each day and use it to the fullest.

This day is a gift from God. How will you use it? Will you celebrate God's gifts and obey His commandments? Will you share words of encouragement and hope with all who cross your path? Will you share the Good News of the risen Christ? Will you trust in the Father and praise His glorious handiwork? The answer to these questions will determine, to a surprising extent, the direction and the quality of your day.

So whatever this day holds for you, begin it and end it with God as your partner and Christ as your Savior. And throughout the day, give thanks to the One who created you and saved you. God's love for you is infinite. Accept it joyously and be thankful.

A TIMELY TIP FROM THE GARDEN OF FAITH

If you don't feel like celebrating, start counting your blessings. Before long, you'll realize that you have plenty of reasons to celebrate.

PROMISES FROM GOD'S WORD

Working together with Him, we also appeal to you: "Don't receive God's grace in vain." For He says: In an acceptable time, I heard you, and in the day of salvation, I helped you. Look, now is the acceptable time; look, now is the day of salvation.

2 CORINTHIANS 6:1-2 HCSB

I must work the works of Him who sent Me while it is day; the night is coming when no one can work.

JOHN 9:4 NKJV

Therefore, get your minds ready for action, being self-disciplined, and set your hope completely on the grace to be brought to you at the revelation of Jesus Christ.

1 PETER 1:13 HCSB

But encourage each other daily, while it is still called today, so that none of you is hardened by sin's deception.

HEBREWS 3:13 HCSB

MORE GREAT IDEAS

Yesterday is the tomb of time, and tomorrow is the womb of time. Only now is yours.

R. G. LEE

Christ is the secret, the source, the substance, the center, and the circumference of all true and lasting gladness.

MRS. CHARLES E. COWMAN

If you can forgive the person you were, accept the person you are, and believe in the person you will become, you are headed for joy. So celebrate your life.

BARBARA JOHNSON

Jesus intended for us to be overwhelmed by the blessings of regular days. He said it was the reason he had come: "I am come that they might have life, and that they might have it more abundantly."

GLORIA GAITHER

Joy comes not from what we have but from what we are.

C. H. SPURGEON

131

If we are ever going to be or do anything for our Lord, now is the time.

VANCE HAVNER

God gave you this glorious day. Don't disappoint Him. Use it for His glory.

MARIE T. FREEMAN

Joy is the direct result of having God's perspective on our daily lives and the effect of loving our Lord enough to obey His commands and trust His promises.

BILL BRIGHT

When the dream of our heart is one that God has planted there, a strange happiness flows into us. At that moment, all of the spiritual resources of the universe are released to help us. Our praying is then at one with the will of God and becomes a channel for the Creator's purposes for us and our world.

CATHERINE MARSHALL

May your day be fashioned with joy, sprinkled with dreams, and touched by the miracle of love.

BARBARA JOHNSON

Submit each day to God,
knowing that He is God
over all your tomorrows.

—

KAY ARTHUR

A PRAYER FOR TODAY

Dear Lord, You have given me another day of life; let me celebrate this day, and let me use it according to Your plan. I come to You today with faith in my heart and praise on my lips. I praise You, Father, for the gift of life and for the friends and family members who make my life rich. Enable me to live each moment to the fullest, totally involved in Your will. Amen

YOUR THOUGHTS ABOUT THE NEED
TO CELEBRATE EACH DAY

_____

_____

_____

_____

_____

_____

_____

_____

_____

MAINTAINING PERSPECTIVE

Make your own attitude that of Christ Jesus.

—

PHILIPPIANS 2:5 HCSB

Sometimes, amid the demands of daily life, we lose perspective. Life seems out of balance, and the pressures of everyday living seem overwhelming. What's needed is a fresh perspective, a restored sense of balance . . . and God.

If a temporary loss of perspective has left you worried, exhausted, or both, it's time to readjust your thought patterns. Negative thoughts are habit-forming; thankfully, so are positive ones. With practice, you can form the habit of focusing on God's priorities and your possibilities. When you do, you'll soon discover that you will spend less time fretting about your challenges and more time praising God for His gifts.

When you call upon the Lord and prayerfully seek His will, He will give you wisdom and perspective. When you make God's priorities your priorities, He will direct your steps and calm your fears. So today and every day hereafter, pray for a sense of balance and perspective. And remember: your thoughts are intensely powerful things, so handle them with care.

A TIMELY TIP FROM THE GARDEN OF FAITH

Keep things in perspective. Your life is an integral part of God's grand plan. So don't become unduly upset over the minor inconveniences of life, and don't worry too much about today's setbacks—they're temporary.

PROMISES FROM GOD'S WORD

Finally brothers, whatever is true, whatever is honorable, whatever is just, whatever is pure, whatever is lovely, whatever is commendable—if there is any moral excellence and if there is any praise—dwell on these things.

PHILIPPIANS 4:8 HCSB

Set your minds on what is above, not on what is on the earth.

COLOSSIANS 3:2 HCSB

Let this mind be in you which was also in Christ Jesus, who, being in the form of God, did not consider it robbery to be equal with God, but made Himself of no reputation, taking the form of a bondservant, and coming in the likeness of men. And being found in appearance as a man, He humbled Himself and became obedient to the point of death, even the death of the cross.

PHILIPPIANS 2:5-8 NKJV

For the word of God is living and powerful, and sharper than any two-edged sword, piercing even to the division of soul and spirit, and of joints and marrow, and is a discerner of the thoughts and intents of the heart.

HEBREWS 4:12 NKJV

MORE GREAT IDEAS

Earthly fears are no fears at all. Answer the big questions of eternity, and the little questions of life fall into perspective.

MAX LUCADO

Like a shadow declining swiftly . . . away . . . like the dew of the morning gone with the heat of the day; like the wind in the treetops, like a wave of the sea, so are our lives on earth when seen in light of eternity.

RUTH BELL GRAHAM

Attitude is the mind's paintbrush; it can color any situation.

BARBARA JOHNSON

When the dream of our heart is one that God has planted there, a strange happiness flows into us. At that moment, all of the spiritual resources of the universe are released to help us. Our praying is then at one with the will of God and becomes a channel for the Creator's purposes for us and our world.

CATHERINE MARSHALL

The proper perspective creates within us a spirit of reaching outside of ourselves with joy and enthusiasm.

LUCI SWINDOLL

What you see and hear depends a good deal on where you are standing; it also depends on what sort of person you are.

C. S. LEWIS

Obey God one step at a time, then the next step will come into view.

CATHERINE MARSHALL

Mature people are not emotionally and spiritually devastated by every mistake they make. They are able to maintain some kind of balance in their lives.

JOYCE MEYER

Joy is the direct result of having God's perspective on our daily lives and the effect of loving our Lord enough to obey His commands and trust His promises.

BILL BRIGHT

Instead of being frustrated
and overwhelmed by all that is
going on in our world,
go to the Lord and ask
Him to give you
His eternal perspective.

—

KAY ARTHUR

A PRAYER FOR TODAY

Dear Lord, give me wisdom and perspective. Guide me according to Your plans for my life and according to Your commandments. And keep me mindful, Dear Lord, that Your truth is—and will forever be—the ultimate truth. Amen

YOUR THOUGHTS ABOUT KEEPING THINGS IN PERSPECTIVE

_____

_____

_____

_____

_____

_____

_____

_____

_____

_____

_____

_____

ACCEPTING GOD'S ABUNDANCE

I am come that they might have life,
and that they might have it more abundantly.

—

JOHN 10:10 KJV

The familiar words of John 10:10 should serve as a daily reminder: Christ came to this earth so that we might experience His abundance, His love, and His gift of eternal life. But Christ does not force Himself upon us; we must claim His gifts for ourselves.

Every woman knows that some days are so busy and so hurried that abundance seems a distant promise. It is not. Every day, we can claim the spiritual abundance that God promises for our lives . . . and we should.

Thomas Brooks spoke for believers of every generation when he observed, "Christ is the sun, and all the watches of our lives should be set by the dial of his motion." Christ, indeed, is the ultimate Savior of mankind and the personal Savior of those who believe in Him. As His servants, we should place Him at the very center of our lives. And, every day that God gives us breath, we should share Christ's love and His abundance with a world that needs both.

A TIMELY TIP FROM THE GARDEN OF FAITH

God wants to shower you with abundance—your job is to let Him.

PROMISES FROM GOD'S WORD

Until now you have asked for nothing in My name. Ask and you will receive, that your joy may be complete.

JOHN 16:24 HCSB

And God is able to make every grace overflow to you, so that in every way, always having everything you need, you may excel in every good work.

2 CORINTHIANS 9:8 HCSB

My cup runs over. Surely goodness and mercy shall follow me all the days of my life; and I will dwell in the house of the Lord forever.

PSALM 23:5-6 NKJV

Come to terms with God and be at peace; in this way good will come to you.

JOB 22:21 HCSB

And He said to them, "Take heed and beware of covetousness, for one's life does not consist in the abundance of the things he possesses."

LUKE 12:15 NKJV

MORE GREAT IDEAS

Yes, we were created for His holy pleasure, but we will ultimately—if not immediately—find much pleasure in His pleasure.

BETH MOORE

It would be wrong to have a "poverty complex," for to think ourselves paupers is to deny either the King's riches or to deny our being His children.

CATHERINE MARSHALL

God's riches are beyond anything we could ask or even dare to imagine! If my life gets gooey and stale, I have no excuse.

BARBARA JOHNSON

God has promised us abundance, peace, and eternal life. These treasures are ours for the asking; all we must do is claim them. One of the great mysteries of life is why on earth do so many of us wait so very long to lay claim to God's gifts?

MARIE T. FREEMAN

Jesus intended for us to be overwhelmed by the blessings of regular days. He said it was the reason he had come: "I am come that they might have life, and that they might have it more abundantly."

GLORIA GAITHER

Get ready for God to show you not only His pleasure, but His approval.

JONI EARECKSON TADA

God is the giver, and we are the receivers. And His richest gifts are bestowed not upon those who do the greatest things, but upon those who accept His abundance and His grace.

HANNAH WHITALL SMITH

The Bible says that being a Christian is not only a great way to die, but it's also the best way to live.

BILL HYBELS

People, places, and things were never meant to give us life. God alone is the author of a fulfilling life.

GARY SMALLEY & JOHN TRENT

God loves you and wants you
to experience peace and life—
abundant and eternal.

—

BILLY GRAHAM

A PRAYER FOR TODAY

Dear Lord, thank You for the joyful, abundant life that is mine through Christ Jesus. Guide me according to Your will, and help me become a woman whose life is a worthy example to others. Give me courage, Lord, to claim the spiritual riches that You have promised, and show me Your plan for my life, today and forever. Amen

YOUR THOUGHTS ABOUT GOD'S ABUNDANCE

_____

_____

_____

_____

_____

_____

_____

_____

_____

_____

_____

HE WANTS YOU TO SERVE

Worship the Lord your God and . . .
serve Him only.

—

MATTHEW 4:10 HCSB

We live in a world that glorifies power, prestige, fame, and money. But the words of Jesus teach us that the most esteemed men and women in this world are not the self-congratulatory leaders of society but are instead the humblest of servants.

Are you willing to become a humble servant for Christ? Are you willing to pitch in and make the world a better place, or are you determined to keep all your blessings to yourself? The answers to these questions will determine the quantity and the quality of the service you render to God and to His children.

Today, you may feel the temptation to take more than you give. You may be tempted to withhold your generosity. Or you may be tempted to build yourself up in the eyes of your friends. Resist those temptations. Instead, serve your friends quietly and without fanfare. Find a need and fill it . . . humbly. Lend a helping hand . . . anonymously. Share a word of kindness . . . with quiet sincerity. As you go about your daily activities, remember that the Savior of all humanity made Himself a servant, and we, as His followers, must do no less.

A TIMELY TIP FROM THE GARDEN OF FAITH

Jesus was a servant, and if you want to follow Him, you must be a servant, too—even when service requires sacrifice.

PROMISES FROM GOD'S WORD

A person should consider us in this way: as servants of Christ and managers of God's mysteries. In this regard, it is expected of managers that each one be found faithful.

1 CORINTHIANS 4:1-2 HCSB

If they serve Him obediently, they will end their days in prosperity and their years in happiness.

JOB 36:11 HCSB

We must do the works of Him who sent Me while it is day. Night is coming when no one can work.

JOHN 9:4 HCSB

Serve the Lord with gladness.

PSALM 100:2 HCSB

If anyone serves Me, let him follow Me; and where I am, there My servant will be also. If anyone serves Me, him My Father will honor.

JOHN 12:26 NKJV

MORE GREAT IDEAS

We are most vulnerable to the piercing winds of doubt when we distance ourselves from the mission and fellowship to which Christ has called us.

JONI EARECKSON TADA

Doing something positive toward another person is a practical approach to feeling good about yourself.

BARBARA JOHNSON

Through our service to others, God wants to influence our world for Him.

VONETTE BRIGHT

God wants us to serve Him with a willing spirit, one that would choose no other way.

BETH MOORE

In the very place where God has put us, whatever its limitations, whatever kind of work it may be, we may indeed serve the Lord Christ.

ELISABETH ELLIOT

So many times we say that we can't serve God because we aren't whatever is needed. We're not talented enough or smart enough or whatever. But if you are in covenant with Jesus Christ, He is responsible for covering your weaknesses, for being your strength. He will give you His abilities for your disabilities!

KAY ARTHUR

God has lots of folks who intend to go to work for him "some day." What He needs is more people who are willing to work for Him today.

MARIE T. FREEMAN

Jesus never asks us to give Him what we don't have. But He does demand that we give Him all we do have if we want to be a part of what He wishes to do in the lives of those around us!

ANNE GRAHAM LOTZ

Hope looks for the good in people, opens doors for people, discovers what can be done to help, lights a candle, does not yield to cynicism. Hope sets people free.

BARBARA JOHNSON

I have discovered that
when I please Christ,
I end up inadvertently serving
others far more effectively.

—

BETH MOORE

A PRAYER FOR TODAY

Dear Lord, in weak moments, I seek to build myself up by placing myself ahead of others. But Your commandment, Father, is that I become a humble servant to those who need my encouragement, my help, and my love. Create in me a servant's heart. And, let be a woman who follows in the footsteps of Your Son Jesus who taught us by example that to be great in Your eyes, Lord, is to serve others humbly, faithfully, and lovingly. Amen

YOUR THOUGHTS ABOUT THE NEED TO SERVE

_____

_____

_____

_____

_____

_____

_____

_____

_____

THE IMPORTANCE OF WORSHIP

*But an hour is coming, and is now here,
when the true worshipers will worship the Father in
spirit and truth. Yes, the Father wants such people to
worship Him. God is Spirit, and those who worship
Him must worship in spirit and truth.*

—

JOHN 4:23-24 HCSB

All of humanity is engaged in worship. The question is not whether we worship, but what we worship. Wise men and women choose to worship God. When they do, they are blessed with a plentiful harvest of joy, peace, and abundance. Other people choose to distance themselves from God by foolishly worshiping things that are intended to bring personal gratification but not spiritual gratification. Such choices often have tragic consequences.

If we place our love for material possessions above our love for God—or if we yield to the countless temptations of this world—we find ourselves engaged in a struggle between good and evil, a clash between God and Satan. Our responses to these struggles have implications that echo throughout our families and throughout our communities.

How can we ensure that we cast our lot with God? We do so, in part, by the practice of regular, purposeful worship in the company of fellow believers. When we worship God faithfully and fervently, we are blessed. When we fail to worship God, for whatever reason, we forfeit the spiritual gifts that He intends for us.

We must worship our Heavenly Father, not just with our words, but also with deeds. We must honor Him, praise Him, and obey Him. As we seek to find purpose and meaning for our lives, we must first seek His purpose and His will. For believers, God comes first. Always first.

PROMISES FROM GOD'S WORD

So that at the name of Jesus every knee should bow—of those who are in heaven and on earth and under the earth—and every tongue should confess that Jesus Christ is Lord, to the glory of God the Father.

PHILIPPIANS 2:10-11 HCSB

And every day they devoted themselves to meeting together in the temple complex, and broke bread from house to house. They ate their food with gladness and simplicity of heart, praising God and having favor with all the people. And every day the Lord added those being saved to them.

ACTS 2:46-47 HCSB

I rejoiced with those who said to me, "Let us go to the house of the Lord."

PSALM 122:1 HCSB

A TIMELY TIP FROM THE GARDEN OF FAITH

The best way to worship God . . . is to worship Him sincerely and often.

MORE GREAT IDEAS

God asks that we worship Him with our concentrated minds as well as with our wills and emotions. A divided and scattered mind is not effective.

CATHERINE MARSHALL

Spiritual worship comes from our very core and is fueled by an awesome reverence and desire for God.

BETH MOORE

To worship Him in truth means to worship Him honestly, without hypocrisy, standing open and transparent before Him.

ANNE GRAHAM LOTZ

God actually delights in and pursues our worship (Proverbs 15:8 & John 4:23).

SHIRLEY DOBSON

In the sanctuary, we discover beauty: the beauty of His presence.

KAY ARTHUR

The deepest level of worship is praising God in spite of pain, thanking God during a trial, trusting him when tempted, surrendering while suffering, and loving him when he seems distant.

RICK WARREN

God has promised to give you all of eternity. The least you can do is give Him one day a week in return.

MARIE T. FREEMAN

Worship is wonder, love, and praise. Not only does it cause us to contemplate and appreciate our holy God, but it gives us vitality, vigor, and a desire to obey Him.

FRANKLIN GRAHAM

Worship is a voluntary act of gratitude offered by the saved to the Savior, by the healed to the Healer, by the delivered to the Deliverer.

MAX LUCADO

Worship is not taught from the pulpit. It must be learned in the heart.

JIM ELLIOT

Praise Him! Praise Him!
Tell of His excellent greatness.
Praise Him! Praise Him!
Ever in joyful song!

—

FANNY CROSBY

A PRAYER FOR TODAY

Lord, let me worship You every day of my life, and let me discover the peace that can be mine when I welcome You into my heart. Amen

YOUR THOUGHTS ABOUT
THE IMPORTANCE OF WORSHIP

CHAPTER
23

DETOURS
ON THE JOURNEY

We are pressured in every way but not crushed;
we are perplexed but not in despair.

—

2 CORINTHIANS 4:8 HCSB

Women of every generation have experienced adversity, and this generation is no different. But, today's women face challenges that previous generations could have scarcely imagined. Thankfully, although the world continues to change, God's love remains constant. And, He remains ready to comfort us and strengthen us whenever we turn to Him.

Psalm 147 promises, "He heals the brokenhearted, and binds their wounds" (v. 3). When we are troubled, we must call upon God, and, in His own time and according to His own plan, He will heal us.

If you are like most women, it is simply a fact of life: from time to time, you worry. You worry about health, about finances, about safety, about relationships, about family, and about countless other challenges of life, some great and some small. Where is the best place to take your worries? Take them to God. Take your troubles to Him, and your fears, and your sorrows. Seek protection from the One who cannot be moved.

A TIMELY TIP FROM THE GARDEN OF FAITH

If you're facing big-time adversity, don't hit the panic button and don't keep everything bottled up inside. Instead of going underground, talk things over with your husband, with your friends, with your pastor, and if necessary, with a trained counselor.

PROMISES FROM GOD'S WORD

I called to the Lord in my distress; I called to my God. From His temple He heard my voice.

2 SAMUEL 22:7 HCSB

I will be with you when you pass through the waters . . . when you walk through the fire . . . the flame will not burn you. For I Yahweh your God, the Holy One of Israel, and your Savior.

ISAIAH 43:2-3 HCSB

Consider it a great joy, my brothers, whenever you experience various trials, knowing that the testing of your faith produces endurance. But endurance must do its complete work, so that you may be mature and complete, lacking nothing.

JAMES 1:2-4 HCSB

When you are in distress and all these things have happened to you, you will return to the Lord your God in later days and obey Him. He will not leave you, destroy you, or forget the covenant with your fathers that He swore to them by oath, because the Lord your God is a compassionate God.

DEUTERONOMY 4:30-31 HCSB

MORE GREAT IDEAS

God will never let you sink under your circumstances. He always provides a safety net and His love always encircles.

BARBARA JOHNSON

Measure the size of the obstacles against the size of God.

BETH MOORE

If all struggles and sufferings were eliminated, the spirit would no more reach maturity than would the child.

ELISABETH ELLIOT

Faith is a strong power, mastering any difficulty in the strength of the Lord who made heaven and earth.

CORRIE TEN BOOM

God helps those who help themselves, but there are times when we are quite incapable of helping ourselves. That's when God stoops down and gathers us in His arms like a mother lifts a sick child, and does for us what we cannot do for ourselves.

RUTH BELL GRAHAM

God whispers to us in our pleasures, speaks in our conscience, but shouts in our pain.

C. S. LEWIS

Even in the winter, even in the midst of the storm, the sun is still there. Somewhere, up above the clouds, it still shines and warms and pulls at the life buried deep inside the brown branches and frozen earth. The sun is there! Spring will come.

GLORIA GAITHER

When problems threaten to engulf us, we must do what believers have always done, turn to the Lord for encouragement and solace. As Psalm 46:1 states, "God is our refuge and strength, an ever-present help in trouble."

SHIRLEY DOBSON

Life will be made or broken at the place where we meet and deal with obstacles.

E. STANLEY JONES

The sermon of your life in tough times ministers to people more powerfully than the most eloquent speaker.

BILL BRIGHT

When faced with adversity
the Christian woman comforts
herself with the knowledge
that all of life's events are
in the hands of God.

—

VONETTE BRIGHT

A PRAYER FOR TODAY

Dear Heavenly Father, when I am troubled, You heal me. When I am afraid, You protect me. When I am discouraged, You lift me up. You are my unending source of strength, Lord; let me turn to You when I am weak. In times of adversity, let me trust Your plan and Your will for my life. And whatever my circumstances, Lord, let me always give the thanks and the glory to You. Amen

YOUR THOUGHTS ABOUT DEALING WITH TOUGH TIMES

ENCOURAGEMENT FOR THE JOURNEY

*I want their hearts to be encouraged and
joined together in love, so that they may have
all the riches of assured understanding,
and have the knowledge of God's mystery—Christ.*

—

COLOSSIANS 2:2 HCSB

A re you a woman who is a continuing source of encouragement to your family and friends? Hopefully so. After all, one of the reasons that God put you here is to serve and encourage other people—starting with the people who live under your roof.

In his letter to the Ephesians, Paul writes, "Do not let any unwholesome talk come out of your mouths, but only what is helpful for building others up according to their needs, that it may benefit those who listen" (4:29 NIV). This passage reminds us that, as Christians, we are instructed to choose our words carefully so as to build others up through wholesome, honest encouragement. How can we build others up? By celebrating their victories and their accomplishments. As the old saying goes, "When someone does something good, applaud—you'll make two people happy."

Today, look for the good in others and celebrate the good that you find. When you do, you'll be a powerful force of encouragement in your corner of the world . . . and a worthy servant to your God.

A TIMELY TIP FROM THE GARDEN OF FAITH

Encouragement is contagious. You can't lift other people up without lifting yourself up, too.

PROMISES FROM GOD'S WORD

Carry one another's burdens; in this way you will fulfill the law of Christ.

GALATIANS 6:2 HCSB

But encourage each other daily, while it is still called today, so that none of you is hardened by sin's deception.

HEBREWS 3:13 HCSB

And let us be concerned about one another in order to promote love and good works.

HEBREWS 10:24 HCSB

Anxiety in a man's heart weighs it down, but a good word cheers it up.

PROVERBS 12:25 HCSB

So then, we must pursue what promotes peace and what builds up one another.

ROMANS 14:19 HCSB

172

MORE GREAT IDEAS

Encouragement starts at home, but it should never end there.

MARIE T. FREEMAN

If I am asked how we are to get rid of discouragements, I can only say, as I have had to say of so many other wrong spiritual habits, we must give them up. It is never worthwhile to argue against discouragement. There is only one argument that can meet it, and that is the argument of God.

HANNAH WHITALL SMITH

The glory of friendship is not the outstretched hand, or the kindly smile, or the joy of companionship. It is the spiritual inspiration that comes to one when he discovers that someone else believes in him and is willing to trust him with his friendship.

CORRIE TEN BOOM

Always stay connected to people and seek out things that bring you joy. Dream with abandon. Pray confidently.

BARBARA JOHNSON

Make it a rule, and pray to God to help you to keep it, never to lie down at night without being able to say: "I have made at least one human being a little wiser, a little happier, or a little better this day."

CHARLES KINGSLEY

A single word, if spoken in a friendly spirit, may be sufficient to turn one from dangerous error.

FANNY CROSBY

Words. Do you fully understand their power? Can any of us really grasp the mighty force behind the things we say? Do we stop and think before we speak, considering the potency of the words we utter?

JONI EARECKSON TADA

One of the ways God refills us after failure is through the blessing of Christian fellowship. Just experiencing the joy of simple activities shared with other children of God can have a healing effect on us.

ANNE GRAHAM LOTZ

He climbs highest who helps another up.

ZIG ZIGLAR

Don't forget that a single sentence,
spoken at the right moment,
can change somebody's
whole perspective on life.
A little encouragement can go
a long, long way.

—

MARIE T. FREEMAN

A PRAYER FOR TODAY

Dear Heavenly Father, because I am Your child, I am blessed. You have loved me eternally, cared for me faithfully, and saved me through the gift of Your Son Jesus. Just as You have lifted me up, Lord, let me lift up others in a spirit of encouragement and optimism and hope. And, if I can help a fellow traveler, even in a small way, Dear Lord, may the glory be Yours. Amen

YOUR THOUGHTS ABOUT THE IMPORTANCE OF ENCOURAGEMENT

_____

_____

_____

_____

_____

_____

_____

_____

_____

_____

CHAPTER
25

ENTHUSIASM FOR THE JOURNEY

Whatever you do, do it enthusiastically,
as something done for the Lord and not for men.

—

COLOSSIANS 3:23 HCSB

Can you truthfully say that you are an enthusiastic person? Are you passionate about your faith, your life, your family, and your future? Hopefully so. But if your zest for life has waned, it is now time to redirect your efforts and recharge your spiritual batteries. And that means refocusing your priorities by putting God first.

Each day is a glorious opportunity to serve God and to do His will. Are you enthused about life, or do you struggle through each day giving scarcely a thought to God's blessings? Are you constantly praising God for His gifts, and are you sharing His Good News with the world? And are you excited about the possibilities for service that God has placed before you, whether at home, at work, or at church? You should be.

Nothing is more important than your wholehearted commitment to your Creator and to His only begotten Son. Your faith must never be an afterthought; it must be your ultimate priority, your ultimate possession, and your ultimate passion. When you become passionate about your faith, you'll become passionate about your life, too.

Norman Vincent Peale advised, "Get absolutely enthralled with something. Throw yourself into it with abandon. Get out of yourself. Be somebody. Do something." His words apply to you. So don't settle for a lukewarm existence. Instead, make the character-building choice to become genuinely involved in life. The world needs your enthusiasm . . . and so do you.

PROMISES FROM GOD'S WORD

I have seen that there is nothing better than for a person to enjoy his activities, because that is his reward. For who can enable him to see what will happen after he dies?

ECCLESIASTES 3:22 HCSB

Do not lack diligence; be fervent in spirit; serve the Lord.

ROMANS 12:11 HCSB

He did it with all his heart. So he prospered.

2 CHRONICLES 31:21 NKJV

Render service with a good attitude, as to the Lord and not to men.

EPHESIANS 6:7 HCSB

A TIMELY TIP FROM THE GARDEN OF FAITH

Don't wait for enthusiasm to find you . . . go looking for it. Look at your life and your relationships as exciting adventures. Don't wait for life to spice up itself; spice things up yourself.

MORE GREAT IDEAS

Your light is the truth of the Gospel message itself as well as your witness as to Who Jesus is and what He has done for you. Don't hide it.

ANNE GRAHAM LOTZ

Don't take hold of a thing unless you want that thing to take hold of you.

E. STANLEY JONES

Living life with a consistent spiritual walk deeply influences those we love most.

VONETTE BRIGHT

Consider every day a new beginning, and always act with the same fervour as on the first day you began.

ST. ANTHONY OF PADUA

One of the great needs in the church today is for every Christian to become enthusiastic about his faith in Jesus Christ.

BILLY GRAHAM

We urgently need people who encourage and inspire us to move toward God and away from the world's enticing pleasures.

JIM CYMBALA

I don't know about you, but I want to do more than survive life—I want to mount up like the eagle and glide over rocky crags, nest in the tallest of trees, dive for nourishment in the deepest of mountain lakes, and soar on the wings of the wind.

BARBARA JOHNSON

Wouldn't it make astounding difference, not only in the quality of the work we do, but also in the satisfaction, even our joy, if we recognized God's gracious gift in every single task?

ELISABETH ELLIOT

God is the giver, and we are the receivers. And His richest gifts are bestowed not upon those who do the greatest things, but upon those who accept His abundance and His grace.

HANNAH WHITALL SMITH

Enthusiasm, like the flu,
is contagious—
we get it from one another.

—

BARBARA JOHNSON

A PRAYER FOR TODAY

Dear Lord, I know that others are watching the way that I live my life. Help me to be an enthusiastic Christian with a faith that is contagious. Amen

YOUR THOUGHTS ABOUT THE REWARDS OF ENTHUSIASM

CHAPTER

26

OPTIMISM NOW

Finally brothers, whatever is true, whatever is honorable, whatever is just, whatever is pure, whatever is lovely, whatever is commendable— if there is any moral excellence and if there is any praise—dwell on these things.

—

PHILIPPIANS 4:8 HCSB

Pessimism and Christianity don't mix. Why? Because Christians have every reason to be optimistic about life here on earth and life eternal. Mrs. Charles E. Cowman advised, "Never yield to gloomy anticipation. Place your hope and confidence in God. He has no record of failure."

Sometimes, despite our trust in God, we may fall into the spiritual traps of worry, frustration, anxiety, or sheer exhaustion, and our hearts become heavy. What's needed is plenty of rest, a large dose of perspective, and God's healing touch, but not necessarily in that order.

Today, make this promise to yourself and keep it: vow to be a hope-filled Christian. Think optimistically about your life, your profession, and your future. Trust your hopes, not your fears. Take time to celebrate God's glorious creation. And then, when you've filled your heart with hope and gladness, share your optimism with others. They'll be better for it, and so will you.

A TIMELY TIP FROM THE GARDEN OF FAITH

Be positive: If your thoughts tend toward the negative end of the spectrum, redirect them. How? You can start by counting your blessings and by thanking your Father in heaven. And while you're at it, train yourself to begin thinking thoughts that are more rational, more accepting, and more upbeat.

PROMISES FROM GOD'S WORD

Make me hear joy and gladness.

PSALM 51:8 NKJV

My cup runs over. Surely goodness and mercy shall follow me all the days of my life; and I will dwell in the house of the Lord Forever.

PSALM 23:5-6 NKJV

But if we hope for what we do not see, we eagerly wait for it with patience.

ROMANS 8:25 HCSB

For God has not given us a spirit of fearfulness, but one of power, love, and sound judgment.

2 TIMOTHY 1:7 HCSB

Be strong and courageous, all you who put your hope in the LORD.

PSALM 31:24 HCSB

MORE GREAT IDEAS

The Christian lifestyle is not one of legalistic do's and don'ts, but one that is positive, attractive, and joyful.

VONETTE BRIGHT

The people whom I have seen succeed best in life have always been cheerful and hopeful people who went about their business with a smile on their faces.

CHARLES KINGSLEY

Don't miss the beautiful colors of the rainbow while you're looking for the pot of gold at the end of it!

BARBARA JOHNSON

If you can't tell whether your glass is half-empty or half-full, you don't need another glass; what you need is better eyesight . . . and a more thankful heart.

MARIE T. FREEMAN

If our hearts have been attuned to God through an abiding faith in Christ, the result will be joyous optimism and good cheer.

BILLY GRAHAM

187

We may run, walk, stumble, drive, or fly, but let us never lose sight of the reason for the journey, or miss a chance to see a rainbow on the way.

GLORIA GAITHER

Keep your feet on the ground, but let your heart soar as high as it will. Refuse to be average or to surrender to the chill of your spiritual environment.

A. W. TOZER

Make the least of all that goes and the most of all that comes. Don't regret what is past. Cherish what you have. Look forward to all that is to come. And most important of all, rely moment by moment on Jesus Christ.

GIGI GRAHAM TCHIVIDJIAN

If our hearts have been attuned to God through an abiding faith in Christ, the result will be joyous optimism and good cheer.

BILLY GRAHAM

Developing a positive attitude
means working continually
to find what is uplifting
and encouraging.

—

BARBARA JOHNSON

A PRAYER FOR TODAY

Dear Lord, I will look for the best in other people, I will expect the best from You, and I will try my best to do my best—today and every day. Amen

YOUR THOUGHTS ABOUT THE REWARDS OF OPTIMISM

_____

_____

_____

_____

_____

_____

_____

_____

_____

_____

_____

_____

_____

CHAPTER
27

YOUR SHEPHERD

The Lord is my shepherd; I shall not want.

—

PSALM 23:1 KJV

Because we are imperfect human beings living imperfect lives, we worry. Even though we, as Christians, have the assurance of salvation—even though we, as believers, have the promise of God's love and protection—we find ourselves fretting over the countless details of everyday life. Jesus understood our concerns, and He addressed them.

In the 6th chapter of Matthew, Jesus makes it clear that the heart of God is a protective, caring heart:

> *Therefore I say to you, do not worry about your life, what you will eat or what you will drink; nor about your body, what you will put on. Is not life more than food and the body more than clothing? Look at the birds of the air, for they neither sow nor reap nor gather into barns; yet your heavenly Father feeds them. Are you not of more value than they? Which of you by worrying can add one cubit to his stature? . . . Therefore do not worry about tomorrow, for tomorrow will worry about its own things. Sufficient for the day is its own trouble. (vv. 25-27, 34)*

Perhaps you are uncertain about your future, your finances, your relationships, or your health. Or perhaps you are simply a "worrier" by nature. If so, make Matthew 6 a regular part of your daily Bible reading. This beautiful passage will remind you that God still sits in His heaven and you are His beloved child. Then, perhaps, you will worry a little less and trust God a little more, and that's as it should be because God is trustworthy . . . and you are protected.

THE 23RD PSALM

The LORD is my shepherd; I shall not want.
He maketh me to lie down in green pastures:
he leadeth me beside the still waters. He restoreth my soul:
he leadeth me in the paths of righteousness for his name's sake.
Yea, though I walk through the valley of the shadow of death,
I will fear no evil: for thou art with me; thy rod and thy staff
they comfort me. Thou preparest a table before me in
the presence of mine enemies: thou anointest my head with
oil; my cup runneth over. Surely goodness and mercy
shall follow me all the days of my life:
and I will dwell in the house of the LORD for ever.

PROMISES FROM GOD'S WORD

Finally, my brethren, be strong in the Lord and in the power of His might. Put on the whole armor of God, that you may be able to stand against the wiles of the devil.

EPHESIANS 6:10-11 NKJV

The Lord your God in your midst, The Mighty One, will save; He will rejoice over you with gladness, He will quiet you with His love, He will rejoice over you with singing.

ZEPHANIAH 3:17 NKJV

I know whom I have believed and am persuaded that He is able to guard what has been entrusted to me until that day.

2 TIMOTHY 1:12 HCSB

A TIMELY TIP FROM THE GARDEN OF FAITH

You are protected by God . . . now and always. The only security that lasts is the security that flows from the loving heart of God.

MORE GREAT IDEAS

Worries carry responsibilities that belong to God, not to you. Worry does not enable us to escape evil; it makes us unfit to cope with it when it comes.

CORRIE TEN BOOM

Only believe, don't fear. Our Master, Jesus, always watches over us, and no matter what the persecution, Jesus will surely overcome it.

LOTTIE MOON

God will never let you sink under your circumstances. He always provides a safety net and His love always encircles.

BARBARA JOHNSON

The Rock of Ages is the great sheltering encirclement.

OSWALD CHAMBERS

A God wise enough to create me and the world I live in is wise enough to watch out for me.

PHILIP YANCEY

We are never out of reach of Satan's devices, so we must never be without the whole armor of God.

WARREN WIERSBE

Our future may look fearfully intimidating, yet we can look up to the Engineer of the Universe, confident that nothing escapes His attention or slips out of the control of those strong hands.

ELISABETH ELLIOT

As sure as God puts his children in the furnace, he will be in the furnace with them.

C. H. SPURGEON

The Lord is the one who travels every mile of the wilderness way as our leader, cheering us, supporting and supplying and fortifying us.

ELISABETH ELLIOT

We will never cease to need our Father—His wisdom, direction, help, and support. We will never outgrow Him. We will always need His grace.

KAY ARTHUR

God never turns away
from the sincere heart.

—

MAX LUCADO

A PRAYER FOR TODAY

Lord, You have promised to protect me, and I will trust You. Today, I will live courageously as I place my hopes, my faith, and life in Your hands. Let my life be a testimony to the transforming power of Your love, Your grace, and Your Son. Amen

YOUR THOUGHTS ABOUT GOD'S PROTECTION

THE RIGHT KIND OF EXAMPLE

*You should be an example to the believers in speech,
in conduct, in love, in faith, in purity.*

—

1 TIMOTHY 4:12 HCSB

Whether we like it or not, all of us are role models. Our friends and family members watch our actions and, as followers of Christ, we are obliged to act accordingly.

What kind of example are you? Are you the kind of woman whose life serves as a genuine example of righteousness? Are you a woman whose behavior serves as a positive role model for young people? Are you the kind of woman whose actions, day in and day out, are based upon kindness, faithfulness, and a love for the Lord? If so, you are not only blessed by God, but you are also a powerful force for good in a world that desperately needs positive influences such as yours.

Corrie ten Boom advised, "Don't worry about what you do not understand. Worry about what you do understand in the Bible but do not live by." And that's sound advice because our families and friends are watching . . . and so, for that matter, is God.

A TIMELY TIP FROM THE GARDEN OF FAITH

God asks you to be a positive example to your family, to your friends, and to the world. The rest is up to you.

PROMISES FROM GOD'S WORD

Do everything without grumbling and arguing, so that you may be blameless and pure.

PHILIPPIANS 2:14–15 HCSB

Set an example of good works yourself, with integrity and dignity in your teaching.

TITUS 2:7 HCSB

For the kingdom of God is not in talk but in power.

1 CORINTHIANS 4:20 HCSB

Therefore since we also have such a large cloud of witnesses surrounding us, let us lay aside every weight and the sin that so easily ensnares us, and run with endurance the race that lies before us.

HEBREWS 12:1 HCSB

You are the light of the world. A city situated on a hill cannot be hidden.

MATTHEW 5:14 HCSB

MORE GREAT IDEAS

In our faith we follow in someone's steps. In our faith we leave footprints to guide others. It's the principle of discipleship.

MAX LUCADO

Our trustworthiness implies His trustworthiness.

BETH MOORE

If we have the true love of God in our hearts, we will show it in our lives. We will not have to go up and down the earth proclaiming it. We will show it in everything we say or do.

D. L. MOODY

Your light is the truth of the Gospel message itself as well as your witness as to Who Jesus is and what He has done for you. Don't hide it.

ANNE GRAHAM LOTZ

You can never separate a leader's actions from his character.

JOHN MAXWELL

In your desire to share the gospel, you may be the only Jesus someone else will ever meet. Be real and be involved with people.

BARBARA JOHNSON

Be to the world a sign that while we as Christians do not have all the answers, we do know and care about the questions.

BILLY GRAHAM

Nothing speaks louder or more powerfully than a life of integrity.

CHARLES SWINDOLL

Our walk counts far more than our talk, always!

GEORGE MUELLER

Among the most joyful people I have known have been some who seem to have had no human reason for joy. The sweet fragrance of Christ has shown through their lives.

ELISABETH ELLIOT

Living life with a consistent
spiritual walk deeply influences
those we love most.

—

VONETTE BRIGHT

A PRAYER FOR TODAY

Dear Lord, help me be a worthy example to my friends and to my family. Let the things that I say and the things that I do show everyone what it means to be a follower of Your Son. Amen

YOUR THOUGHTS ABOUT THE IMPORTANCE OF SETTING A GOOD EXAMPLE

ABOVE AND BEYOND WORRY

*Don't worry about your life, what you will eat or
what you will drink; or about your body,
what you will wear. Isn't life more than food
and the body more than clothing?*

—

MATTHEW 6:25 HCSB

If you are like most women, it is simply a fact of life: from time to time, you worry. You worry about health, about finances, about safety, about relationships, about family, and about countless other challenges of life, some great and some small. Where is the best place to take your worries? Take them to God. Take your troubles to Him, and your fears, and your sorrows.

Barbara Johnson correctly observed, "Worry is the senseless process of cluttering up tomorrow's opportunities with leftover problems from today." So if you'd like to make the most out of this day (and every one hereafter), turn your worries over to a Power greater than yourself . . . and spend your valuable time and energy solving the problems you can fix . . . while trusting God to do the rest.

A TIMELY TIP FROM THE GARDEN OF FAITH

An important part of becoming a more mature Christian is learning to worry less and to trust God more.

PROMISES FROM GOD'S WORD

Don't worry about anything, but in everything, through prayer and petition with thanksgiving, let your requests be made known to God.

PHILIPPIANS 4:6 HCSB

Therefore don't worry about tomorrow, because tomorrow will worry about itself. Each day has enough trouble of its own.

MATTHEW 6:34 HCSB

Yea, though I walk through the valley of the shadow of death, I will fear no evil: for thou art with me; thy rod and thy staff they comfort me.

PSALM 23:4 KJV

I will be with you when you pass through the waters . . . when you walk through the fire . . . the flame will not burn you. For I Yahweh your God, the Holy One of Israel, and your Savior.

ISAIAH 43:2-3 HCSB

Anxiety in a man's heart weighs it down, but a good word cheers it up.

PROVERBS 12:25 HCSB

MORE GREAT IDEAS

We are not called to be burden-bearers, but cross-bearers and light-bearers. We must cast our burdens on the Lord.

CORRIE TEN BOOM

When there is perplexity there is always guidance—not always at the moment we ask, but in good time, which is God's time. There is no need to fret and stew.

ELISABETH ELLIOT

Anxiety may be natural and normal for the world, but it is not to be part of a believer's lifestyle.

KAY ARTHUR

When we do what is right, we have contentment, peace, and happiness.

BEVERLY LAHAYE

Never yield to gloomy anticipation. Place your hope and confidence in God. He has no record of failure.

MRS. CHARLES E. COWMAN

Today is mine. Tomorrow is none of my business. If I peer anxiously into the fog of the future, I will strain my spiritual eyes so that I will not see clearly what is required of me now.

ELISABETH ELLIOTT

This life of faith, then, consists in just this—being a child in the Father's house. Let the ways of childish confidence and freedom from care, which so please you and win your heart when you observe your own little ones, teach you what you should be in your attitude toward God.

HANNAH WHITALL SMITH

There is something about having endured great loss that brings purity of purpose and strength of character.

BARBARA JOHNSON

Worship and worry cannot live in the same heart; they are mutually exclusive.

RUTH BELL GRAHAM

Worry is a cycle of inefficient
thoughts whirling around
a center of fear.

—

CORRIE TEN BOOM

A PRAYER FOR TODAY

Dear Lord, wherever I find myself, let me celebrate more and worry less. When my faith begins to waver, help me to trust You more. Then, with praise on my lips and the love of Your Son in my heart, let me live courageously, faithfully, prayerfully, and thankfully this day and every day. Amen

YOUR THOUGHTS ABOUT TRUSTING GOD

_____

_____

_____

_____

_____

_____

_____

_____

_____

_____

_____

_____

THE GIFT OF ETERNAL LIFE

*And this is the testimony: God has given us
eternal life, and this life is in His Son.
The one who has the Son has life.
The one who doesn't have the Son of God
does not have life.*

—

1 JOHN 5:11-12 HCSB

Your life here on earth is merely a preparation for a far different life to come: the eternal life that God promises to those who welcome His Son into their hearts.

As a mere mortal, your vision for the future is finite. God's vision is not burdened by such limitations: His plans extend throughout all eternity. Thus, God's plans for you are not limited to the ups and downs of everyday life. Your Heavenly Father has bigger things in mind . . . much bigger things.

How marvelous it is that God became a man and walked among us. Had He not chosen to do so, we might feel removed from a distant Creator. But ours is not a distant God. Ours is a God who understands—far better than we ever could—the essence of what it means to be human.

God understands our hopes, our fears, and our temptations. He understands what it means to be angry and what it costs to forgive. He knows the heart, the conscience, and the soul of every person who has ever lived, including you.

As you struggle with the inevitable hardships and occasional disappointments of life, remember that God has invited you to accept His abundance not only for today but also for all eternity. So keep things in perspective. Although you will inevitably encounter occasional defeats in this world, you'll have all eternity to celebrate the ultimate victory in the next.

PROMISES FROM GOD'S WORD

I have written these things to you who believe in the name of the Son of God, so that you may know that you have eternal life.

1 JOHN 5:13 HCSB

Jesus said to her, "I am the resurrection and the life. The one who believes in Me, even if he dies, will live. Everyone who lives and believes in Me will never die—ever. Do you believe this?"

JOHN 11:25-26 HCSB

Pursue righteousness, godliness, faith, love, endurance, and gentleness. Fight the good fight for the faith; take hold of eternal life, to which you were called and have made a good confession before many witnesses.

1 TIMOTHY 6:11-12 HCSB

A TIMELY TIP FROM THE GARDEN OF FAITH

People love talking about religion, and everybody has their own opinions, but ultimately only one opinion counts . . . God's. Think about God's promise of eternal life—and what that promise means to you.

215

MORE GREAT IDEAS

God has promised us abundance, peace, and eternal life. These treasures are ours for the asking; all we must do is claim them. One of the great mysteries of life is why on earth do so many of us wait so very long to lay claim to God's gifts?

MARIE T. FREEMAN

I can still hardly believe it. I, with shriveled, bent fingers, atrophied muscles, gnarled knees, and no feeling from the shoulders down, will one day have a new body— light, bright and clothed in righteousness—powerful and dazzling.

JONI EARECKSON TADA

Your choice to either receive or reject the Lord Jesus Christ will determine where you spend eternity.

ANNE GRAHAM LOTZ

And because we know Christ is alive, we have hope for the present and hope for life beyond the grave.

BILLY GRAHAM

If you are a believer, your judgment will not determine your eternal destiny. Christ's finished work on Calvary was applied to you the moment you accepted Christ as Savior.

BETH MOORE

God is not saving the world; it is done. Our business is to get men and women to realize it.

OSWALD CHAMBERS

The gift of God is eternal life, spiritual life, abundant life through faith in Jesus Christ, the Living Word of God.

ANNE GRAHAM LOTZ

Let us see the victorious Jesus, the conqueror of the tomb, the one who defied death. And let us be reminded that we, too, will be granted the same victory.

MAX LUCADO

Salvation is the exchange of all that you are for all that Christ is.

JOHN MACARTHUR

The unfolding of our friendship
with the Father will be
a never-ending revelation
stretching on into eternity.

—

CATHERINE MARSHALL

A PRAYER FOR TODAY

I know, Lord, that this world is not my home; I am only here for a brief while. And, You have given me the priceless gift of eternal life through Your Son Jesus. Keep the hope of heaven fresh in my heart, and, while I am in this world, help me to pass through it with faith in my heart and praise on my lips . . . for You. Amen

YOUR THOUGHTS ABOUT GOD'S PROMISE OF ETERNAL LIFE

"*Daughter,*" *He said to her,*
"*your faith has made you well.*
Go in peace."

—

LUKE 8:48 HCSB

MORE FROM
GOD'S WORD

ANGER

A patient person [shows] great understanding, but a quick-tempered one promotes foolishness.

PROVERBS 14:29 HCSB

But now you must also put away all the following: anger, wrath, malice, slander, and filthy language from your mouth.

COLOSSIANS 3:8 HCSB

Don't let your spirit rush to be angry, for anger abides in the heart of fools.

ECCLESIASTES 7:9 HCSB

All bitterness, anger and wrath, insult and slander must be removed from you, along with all wickedness. And be kind and compassionate to one another, forgiving one another, just as God also forgave you in Christ.

EPHESIANS 4:31-32 HCSB

Everyone must be quick to hear, slow to speak, and slow to anger, for man's anger does not accomplish God's righteousness.

JAMES 1:19-20 HCSB

ATTITUDE

For the word of God is living and effective and sharper than any two-edged sword, penetrating as far as to divide soul, spirit, joints, and marrow; it is a judge of the ideas and thoughts of the heart.

HEBREWS 4:12 HCSB

Make your own attitude that of Christ Jesus.

PHILIPPIANS 2:5 HCSB

Finally brothers, whatever is true, whatever is honorable, whatever is just, whatever is pure, whatever is lovely, whatever is commendable—if there is any moral excellence and if there is any praise—dwell on these things.

PHILIPPIANS 4:8 HCSB

Set your minds on what is above, not on what is on the earth.

COLOSSIANS 3:2 HCSB

A cheerful heart has a continual feast.

PROVERBS 15:15 HCSB

CELEBRATION

This is the day the LORD has made; we will rejoice and be glad in it.

PSALM 118:24 NKJV

Rejoice in the Lord always. I will say it again: Rejoice!

PHILIPPIANS 4:4 HCSB

David and the whole house of Israel were celebrating before the Lord.

2 SAMUEL 6:5 HCSB

Their sorrow was turned into rejoicing and their mourning into a holiday. They were to be days of feasting, rejoicing, and of sending gifts to one another and the poor.

ESTHER 9:22 HCSB

At the dedication of the wall of Jerusalem, they sent for the Levites wherever they lived and brought them to Jerusalem to celebrate the joyous dedication with thanksgiving and singing accompanied by cymbals, harps, and lyres.

NEHEMIAH 12:27 HCSB

GRACE

For the law was given through Moses; grace and truth came through Jesus Christ.

JOHN 1:17 HCSB

Therefore let us approach the throne of grace with boldness, so that we may receive mercy and find grace to help us at the proper time.

HEBREWS 4:16 HCSB

Therefore, since we are receiving a kingdom that cannot be shaken, let us hold on to grace. By it, we may serve God acceptably, with reverence and awe.

HEBREWS 12:28 HCSB

For by grace you are saved through faith, and this is not from yourselves; it is God's gift—not from works, so that no one can boast.

EPHESIANS 2:8-9 HCSB

You, therefore, my child, be strong in the grace that is in Christ Jesus.

2 TIMOTHY 2:1 HCSB

HAPPINESS

How happy are those whose way is blameless, who live according to the law of the Lord! Happy are those who keep His decrees and seek Him with all their heart.

PSALM 119:1-2 HCSB

If they serve Him obediently, they will end their days in prosperity and their years in happiness.

JOB 36:11 HCSB

The one who understands a matter finds success, and the one who trusts in the Lord will be happy.

PROVERBS 16:20 HCSB

Happy are the people whose strength is in You, whose hearts are set on pilgrimage.

PSALM 84:5 HCSB

A joyful heart is good medicine, but a broken spirit dries up the bones.

PROVERBS 17:22 HCSB

LOVING GOD

He said to him, "You shall love the Lord your God with all your heart, with all your soul, and with all your mind. This is the greatest and most important commandment."

MATTHEW 22:37-38 HCSB

And we have this command from Him: the one who loves God must also love his brother.

1 JOHN 4:21 HCSB

For this is the love of God, that we keep His commandments. And His commandments are not burdensome.

1 JOHN 5:3 NKJV

Love the Lord your God with all your heart, with all your soul, and with all your strength. These words that I am giving you today are to be in your heart. Repeat them to your children. Talk about them when you sit in your house and when you walk along the road, when you lie down and when you get up.

DEUTERONOMY 6:5-7 HCSB

We love Him because He first loved us.

1 JOHN 4:19 NKJV

MATERIALISM

And He told them, "Watch out and be on guard against all greed, because one's life is not in the abundance of his possessions."

LUKE 12:15 HCSB

For what does it benefit a man to gain the whole world yet lose his life? What can a man give in exchange for his life?

MARK 8:36-37 HCSB

Don't collect for yourselves treasures on earth, where moth and rust destroy and where thieves break in and steal. But collect for yourselves treasures in heaven, where neither moth nor rust destroys, and where thieves don't break in and steal. For where your treasure is, there your heart will be also.

MATTHEW 6:19-21 HCSB

For the mind-set of the flesh is death, but the mind-set of the Spirit is life and peace.

ROMANS 8:6 HCSB

OBEDIENCE

Therefore, get your minds ready for action, being self-disciplined, and set your hope completely on the grace to be brought to you at the revelation of Jesus Christ. As obedient children, do not be conformed to the desires of your former ignorance but, as the One who called you is holy, you also are to be holy in all your conduct.

1 PETER 1:13-15 HCSB

And the world with its lust is passing away, but the one who does God's will remains forever.

1 JOHN 2:17 HCSB

Now by this we know that we know Him, if we keep His commandments. . . . But whoever keeps His word, truly the love of God is perfected in him. By this we know that we are in Him. He who says he abides in Him ought himself also to walk just as He walked.

1 JOHN 2:3, 5-6 NKJV

For this is what love for God is: to keep His commands. Now His commands are not a burden, because whatever has been born of God conquers the world. This is the victory that has conquered the world: our faith.

1 JOHN 5:3-4 HCSB

229

PRIDE

Your eyes are set against the proud—You humble them.

2 SAMUEL 22:28 HCSB

Do not love the world or the things that belong to the world. If anyone loves the world, love for the Father is not in him. Because everything that belongs to the world—the lust of the flesh, the lust of the eyes, and the pride in one's lifestyle—is not from the Father, but is from the world.

1 JOHN 2:15-16 HCSB

But as for me, I will never boast about anything except the cross of our Lord Jesus Christ, through whom the world has been crucified to me, and I to the world.

GALATIANS 6:14 HCSB

The arrogant will stumble and fall with no one to pick him up.

JEREMIAH 50:32 HCSB

Do nothing out of rivalry or conceit, but in humility consider others as more important than yourselves.

PHILIPPIANS 2:3 HCSB

PROBLEMS

Your heart must not be troubled. Believe in God; believe also in Me.

JOHN 14:1 HCSB

God is our refuge and strength, a very present help in trouble.

PSALM 46:1 NKJV

I will be with you when you pass through the waters . . . when you walk through the fire . . . the flame will not burn you. For I the Lord your God, the Holy One of Israel, and your Savior.

ISAIAH 43:2-3 HCSB

The righteous is rescued from trouble; in his place, the wicked goes in.

PROVERBS 11:8 HCSB

Then they cried out to the Lord in their trouble, and He saved them out of their distresses.

PSALM 107:13 NKJV

RIGHTEOUSNESS

Because the eyes of the Lord are on the righteous and His ears are open to their request. But the face of the Lord is against those who do evil.

1 PETER 3:12 HCSB

Therefore, come out from among them and be separate, says the Lord; do not touch any unclean thing, and I will welcome you.

2 CORINTHIANS 6:17 HCSB

Flee from youthful passions, and pursue righteousness, faith, love, and peace, along with those who call on the Lord from a pure heart.

2 TIMOTHY 2:22 HCSB

And now, Israel, what does the Lord your God ask of you except to fear the Lord your God by walking in all His ways, to love Him, and to worship the Lord your God with all your heart and all your soul?

DEUTERONOMY 10:12 HCSB

STRESS

Cast your burden on the Lord, and He shall sustain you; He shall never permit the righteous to be moved.

PSALM 55:22 NKJV

Your heart must not be troubled. Believe in God; believe also in Me.

JOHN 14:1 HCSB

Then they cried out to the Lord in their trouble, and He saved them out of their distresses.

PSALM 107:13 NKJV

For You, O God, have tested us; You have refined us as silver is refined. You brought us into the net; You laid affliction on our backs. You have caused men to ride over our heads; we went through fire and through water; but You brought us out to rich fulfillment.

PSALM 66:10–12 NKJV

Rejoice in hope; be patient in affliction; be persistent in prayer.

ROMANS 12:12 HCSB

TALENTS

Do not neglect the gift that is in you.

1 TIMOTHY 4:14 HCSB

Each one has his own gift from God, one in this manner and another in that.

1 CORINTHIANS 7:7 NKJV

So he who had received five talents came and brought five other talents, saying, "Lord, you delivered to me five talents; look, I have gained five more talents besides them." His lord said to him, "Well done, good and faithful servant; you were faithful over a few things, I will make you ruler over many things. Enter into the joy of your lord."

MATTHEW 25:20-21 NKJV

I remind you to keep ablaze the gift of God that is in you.

2 TIMOTHY 1:6 HCSB

Based on the gift they have received, everyone should use it to serve others, as good managers of the varied grace of God.

1 PETER 4:10 HCSB

TEACHING

Set an example of good works yourself, with integrity and dignity in your teaching.

TITUS 2:7 HCSB

Teach a youth about the way he should go; even when he is old he will not depart from it.

PROVERBS 22:6 HCSB

According to the grace given to us, we have different gifts: If prophecy, use it according to the standard of faith; if service, in service; if teaching, in teaching; if exhorting, in exhortation; giving, with generosity; leading, with diligence; showing mercy, with cheerfulness.

ROMANS 12:6-8 HCSB

Be conscientious about yourself and your teaching; persevere in these things, for by doing this you will save both yourself and your hearers.

1 TIMOTHY 4:13 HCSB

TEMPTATION

No temptation has overtaken you except what is common to humanity. God is faithful and He will not allow you to be tempted beyond what you are able, but with the temptation He will also provide a way of escape, so that you are able to bear it.

1 CORINTHIANS 10:13 HCSB

Do not be deceived: "Bad company corrupts good morals."

1 CORINTHIANS 15:33 HCSB

Be sober! Be on the alert! Your adversary the Devil is prowling around like a roaring lion, looking for anyone he can devour.

1 PETER 5:8 HCSB

The Lord knows how to deliver the godly out of temptations.

2 PETER 2:9 NKJV

Put on the full armor of God so that you can stand against the tactics of the Devil.

EPHESIANS 6:11 HCSB

YOUR TESTIMONY

But sanctify the Lord God in your hearts, and always be ready to give a defense to everyone who asks you a reason for the hope that is in you.

1 PETER 3:15 HCSB

You are the light of the world. A city that is set on a hill cannot be hidden. Nor do they light a lamp and put it under a basket, but on a lampstand, and it gives light to all who are in the house. Let your light so shine before men, that they may see your good works and glorify your Father in heaven.

MATTHEW 5:14–16 NKJV

Whatever I tell you in the dark, speak in the light; and what you hear in the ear, preach on the housetops.

MATTHEW 10:27 NKJV

And I say to you, anyone who acknowledges Me before men, the Son of Man will also acknowledge him before the angels of God; but whoever denies Me before men will be denied before the angels of God.

LUKE 12:8-9 HCSB

TRUTH

For everyone who practices wicked things hates the light and avoids it, so that his deeds may not be exposed. But anyone who lives by the truth comes to the light, so that his works may be shown to be accomplished by God.

JOHN 3:20–21 HCSB

Be diligent to present yourself approved to God, a worker who doesn't need to be ashamed, correctly teaching the word of truth.

2 TIMOTHY 2:15 HCSB

I have no greater joy than this: to hear that my children are walking in the truth.

3 JOHN 1:4 HCSB

You have already heard about this hope in the message of truth, the gospel that has come to you. It is bearing fruit and growing all over the world, just as it has among you since the day you heard it and recognized God's grace in the truth.

COLOSSIANS 1:5-6 HCSB

WISDOM

Therefore, everyone who hears these words of Mine and acts on them will be like a sensible man who built his house on the rock. The rain fell, the rivers rose, and the winds blew and pounded that house. Yet it didn't collapse, because its foundation was on the rock.

MATTHEW 7:24–25 HCSB

But from Him you are in Christ Jesus, who for us became wisdom from God, as well as righteousness, sanctification, and redemption.

1 CORINTHIANS 1:30 HCSB

For God has not given us a spirit of fearfulness, but one of power, love, and sound judgment.

2 TIMOTHY 1:7 HCSB

Now if any of you lacks wisdom, he should ask God, who gives to all generously and without criticizing, and it will be given to him.

JAMES 1:5 HCSB

WORLDLINESS

Pure and undefiled religion before our God and Father is this: to look after orphans and widows in their distress and to keep oneself unstained by the world.

JAMES 1:27 HCSB

Now we have not received the spirit of the world, but the Spirit who is from God, in order to know what has been freely given to us by God.

1 CORINTHIANS 2:12 HCSB

No one should deceive himself. If anyone among you thinks he is wise in this age, he must become foolish so that he can become wise. For the wisdom of this world is foolishness with God, since it is written: He catches the wise in their craftiness.

1 CORINTHIANS 3:18-19 HCSB

Do not love the world or the things that belong to the world. If anyone loves the world, love for the Father is not in him.

1 JOHN 2:15 HCSB

Do not have other gods besides Me.

EXODUS 20:3 HCSB